WOODWORKER'S GUIDE TO

Veneering
& Inlay

WOODWORKER'S GUIDE TO

Veneering & Inlay

JONATHAN BENSON

FOX CHAPEL
PUBLISHING

Woodworker's Guide to Veneering and Inlay is an original work, first published in 2008
by Fox Chapel Publishing Company, Inc. No part of this publication may be reproduced, stored
in a retrieval system or transmitted, in any form or by any means, electronic, mechanical,
photocopying, recording or otherwise, without the prior written permission of the publishers
and copyright holders.

ISBN 978-1-56523-346-1

Publisher's Cataloging-in-Publication Data

Benson, Jonathan.

      Woodworker's guide to veneering & inlay / Jonathan Benson. -- East
Petersburg, PA : Fox Chapel Publishing, c2008.

          p. ; cm.

      ISBN: 978-1-56523-346-1
      Includes bibliographical references and index.

          1. Veneers and veneering. 2. Marquetry. 3.Woodwork. I. Title.
   II. Title: Veneering and inlay.

TS870 .B46 2008
674/.833--dc22   0711

To learn more about the other great books from
Fox Chapel Publishing, or to find a retailer near you,
call toll-free 800-457-9112 or visit us at *www.FoxChapelPublishing.com*.

Printed in Singapore
Fifth printing

Dedication

To Sherry

Acknowledgments

During the past three decades, I have been lucky enough to work at a craft I love, to continue to explore new ideas in the studio, and to then pass on that knowledge. I want to thank the many students I have had for their thoughtful questions and new insights, which have taught me so much. I would also like to thank my clients for giving me the freedom to push the boundaries of my work and move it into new areas. Finally, I would like to thank Sherry, my wife, for her love and support during the past 20 years.

This book would not have been possible without John Kelsey's thoughtful editing and extensive knowledge about the woodworking field. I would also like to thank those who contributed material for the production of this book, including Silas Kopf, Northhampton, Massachusetts; Frank Pollaro, Pollaro Custom Furniture Inc., Union, New Jersey; Dave Bilger, B&B Rare Woods; Michael Erath, Erath Veneers; Dave Boykin, Boykin Pearce Associates, Denver, Colorado; Mike Bray, Berkeley, California; and *Woodwork Magazine.*

—Jonathan Benson, West Des Moines, Iowa, April 2007

Contents

CHAPTER 1

Veneering Then & Now

A wood veneer is an attractive but thin slice of wood that can be glued
onto a furniture surface or wall panel, creating a rich look for very little
expenditure of expensive material. Veneering is an old process that has
changed and developed along with advances in wood processing and
cutting. Historically, veneer was used to decorate the very finest furniture;
in recent times, it has also been used to disguise some of the worst.
Today, it is still possible to produce very fine veneered furniture using
basic woodworking tools.

Desert Sun Sideboard
by Jonathan Benson
combines vintage Brazilian
rosewood, curly maple,
and ebony veneers.
The 36" x 62" x 22"
sideboard was created
using the simple tools
and techniques covered
in this book.

Historical background

Veneers have been used in woodworking for more than 5,500 years. Examples of veneered pieces dating back to at least 3500 BC have been discovered in the pyramids of ancient Egypt. Hieroglyphics and frescoes created around 1950 BC depict workers cutting, joining, and gluing down sheets of veneer using stones as weights for clamping. The veneers were cut with an adze, a tool resembling an ax with its blade turned perpendicular to the handle. This process produced veneers that were rough, uneven, and about ¼" thick.

As technology progressed, it became possible to make thinner veneers. In Roman times, an iron-bladed pit saw was used. One worker stood in a pit below a log while another worker stood above, each pulling opposite ends of a large saw. The Romans also developed smaller bow-type saws, which could be used by one or two people. Sawn veneers could be much thinner than adzed veneers, close to ⅛" thick. Like adzed veneers, these early sawn veneers remained uneven and required much leveling and smoothing to create an even surface. Because these processes were

Figure 1-2. A wet bar wall, made with quilted makoré panels and cabinets, pomele sapele bent-laminated doors, and a granite counter top, was designed by Dave Boykin and made by the three-man shop of Boykin-Pearce Associates, Denver, Colorado. (Photo courtesy Dave Boykin.)

labor intensive, veneers could only be used in the highest applications.

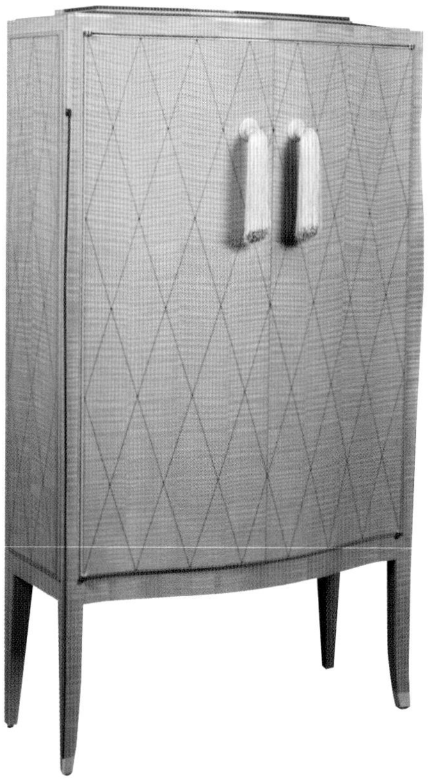

Just like craftsmen today, early craftsmen had good reason to go to such trouble to fabricate veneers. In ancient Egypt, fine woods of interesting and contrasting figure had to be transported great distances, making them scarce. Cutting the wood into thin layers enabled it to cover more surface area. Also, rare and highly prized burls, large knotty growths found in many species of woods, will check, crack, and warp unless sawn very thin (**Figure 1-3**). Additionally, thin woods can be arranged and combined in intricate patterns, regardless of grain direction or species, without problems due to wood movement (see Chapter 2).

When circular saws came into use during the Industrial Revolution, veneers of ¹⁄₁₆" could be produced in large quantities. Veneer began to be used on a much greater scale. More people than ever before could own these inexpensive, mass-produced goods. Unfortunately, at this same time, veneer came to be associated with cheap, shoddy construction. The idea of a fine veneer covering over a cheap interior has been associated with the process ever since. Dictionaries today define veneer as "to disguise with superficial polish" or a "false show of charm" (Webster's Dictionary, New Edition).

Figure 1-1. A 48" x 22" x 12" Art Deco chiffonier in curly maple is a classic 1930s Ruhlmann reproduction by Pollaro Custom Furniture Inc., Union, New Jersey. (Photo courtesy Frank Pollaro.)

Figure 1-3. *Ziggurat Chest of Drawers,* 60" x 24" x 18", by furniture artist Silas Kopf of Northhampton, Massachusetts, features burl veneers with mother-of-pearl inlay banding. (Photo courtesy Silas Kopf.)

The middle class grew tremendously as labor shifted from working the land to working in factories. Technology continued to advance and veneer became ever thinner. With the incorporation of the mechanized knife in the early 20th century, veneer could be sliced to $\frac{1}{32}$" or less. (Today, most U.S. veneer is $\frac{1}{28}$".) This was a huge advance in the efficient use of woods. The veneer was cut thinner, allowing it to cover more surface area, and the saw kerf (waste from the thickness of the saw blade itself) was eliminated. Far more veneer with a matching pattern could be produced, allowing for the coverage of larger areas, including entire rooms (**Figure 1-2**), with the same uniform pattern.

Then, due to the popularity of exotic woods during the first half of the 20th century, some of the finest furniture being produced was made using veneers (**Figure 1-1**). Consequently, during the last 200 years, veneer has lived a dual existence as the best and worst that wood furniture design has to offer. Contemporary furniture artists have again turned to veneer for both the beauty and luxury it offers as well as its economy and practicality (**Figure 1-4**).

Figure 1-4. A very practical set of three nesting tables by Jonathan Benson combines purpleheart veneer with stained curly maple turnings (20" x 26" x 20"). Although it might have been possible to make the curved side panels in solid wood instead of laminated veneers, the cost would have been prohibitive.

Advantages of veneer

With the rapid rate of deforestation and the near disappearance of an increasing number of tree species, use as veneers may be the only alternative left for many types of woods. Already, many species and rare figure configurations are only available in veneer form (see page 2). Some exceptionally rare species, such as premium-grade fiddleback makoré, may only appear on the market as one or two large veneer logs every few years.

The yield advantage of using veneer is tremendous. Take a given log and rough-cut 1"-thick boards from it. The lumber, dried and planed on both sides, yields a ¾"-thick board that will cover one square foot of surface area for every board foot of lumber sawn. Take the same log and cut it into $\frac{1}{30}$" to $\frac{1}{40}$" veneers, and it will cover 30 to 40 times as much surface area. Considering that, per square foot, the retail price of 1"-thick lumber is often only two or three times the cost of veneer, it is obvious why the best logs go to the veneer mill.

There are also environmental advantages to consider. Less lumber grown in tropical rainforests is needed to cover the same surface area when sawn as veneer. Renewable and waste materials, including recycled industrial waste, can be used as a substrate (see Chapter 4, page 44). Many companies are starting to use non-toxic, soy-based glues to manufacture particleboard, fiberboard, and plywood, all of which can be used as veneer substrates.

But the visual advantages of veneer may be the most important to designers. Veneers make it possible to combine different woods in an infinite number of ways, regardless of grain direction. That makes them "omni-directional"—both movement

Figure 1-5.
Silas Kopf: *Tulips and Bees* side table (54" x 20" x 35") combines marquetry in the floral doors and the bees, with parquetry in the assembly of blocks containing the bee motif itself.

across the grain and movement due to differing densities of various species are eliminated once the veneer has been properly glued down to the appropriate substrate. The veneer is just too thin to move in any direction, regardless of seasonal weather changes. The idea can be taken to beautiful extremes, as in the pictures created by marquetry and the geometric patterns of parquetry (see **Figure 1-5**, for example). In addition to marquetry and parquetry, veneer patterns commonly include book-matching, four-way matching, and radial matching. In book-matching, the leaves of veneer open like a book and the pattern reverses from one leaf to the next. In a four-way match, the book-match occurs both side-by-side and top-to-bottom, like a folded piece of paper. In a radial match, triangles of matched veneer fit together around a common center like a sunburst. More complex patterns are based on the three basic ones.

Figure 1-6. Treefrog Veneers manufactures a variety of exotic-looking laminate sheets to be used like wood veneers.

Figure 1-7. The curvy base of Jonathan Benson's *W Table* is made by bending and gluing fiddledback makoré veneer and combining curly maple elements (17" x 44" x 22").

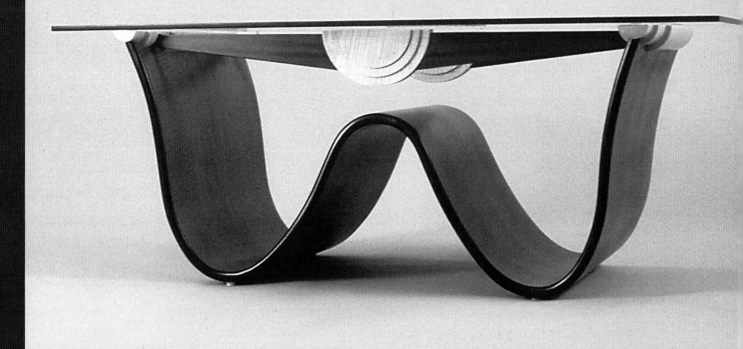

Figure 1-8. Veneer is flexible and can easily be laminated into curved furniture forms. *Constructivist Coffee Table,* by Jonathan Benson, includes walnut, cherry, and granite (17" x 44" x 22").

Newer veneer materials, which can help conserve precious tropical lumber, are always coming on the market. They are made from less scarce and sustainable species of wood, as well as from synthetic materials made to look like rare woods. Other products have intricately patterned surfaces that do not resemble wood at all and can be produced in almost any color. Some have a herringbone or other pleasing pattern. The materials can completely change what a wood surface looks like, and are applied in much the same manner as traditional veneers, often combined with other wood veneers and solid wood (**Figure 1-6**).

Because a sheet of veneer is extremely flexible, all of the patterns, book-matches, and inlays discussed in this book can be applied to curved surfaces (demonstrated by the curved mirror project in Chapter 12). In fact, modern veneer

Figure 1-9. *Dining Table* by Jonathan Benson is made of holly wood and Swiss pearwood veneer, stained and painted wood, and glass (56" x 28").

Figure 1-10. *Sideboard* by Jonathan Benson is vintage Brazilian rosewood veneer and curly maple with tambour doors (36" x 50" x 18").

Figure 1-11. Jonathan Benson's *Pyramid Pedestal* (37" x 15" x 15") has a bubinga base, vintage African satinwood sides, cocobolo and bubinga trim, a granite top, and a light to illuminate the gold-plated capstone made by jewelry artist Matha Benson.

Figure 1-12. *Hall Table* by Jonathan Benson features fiddleback makoré, curly maple, and glass (32" x 48" x 18").

Figure 1-13. *Samovar Wall Shelf*, with holly and Swiss pearwood veneers by Jonathan Benson, combines painted and stained woods (36" x 56" x 12").

gluing and pressing techniques make it relatively simple to veneer over curved surfaces, as well as to create curved pieces made entirely of veneer (**Figures 1-7** and **1-8**).

The ability to properly handle, cut, match, and attach veneers can open up an entirely new range of ideas to woodcrafters of any skill level. At the same time, a lot of wood can be saved by using veneers. Most of the veneering processes covered in this book do not take a huge investment of either shop space or money. A small shop or an individual can go a long way using the basic tools most woodworkers already have. The addition of a screw-type or vacuum-bag veneer press opens up even more possibilities (see **Figures 1-9** through **1-16**). I will also cover more complex and production-oriented processes for shops that do a lot of veneer work. Anyone with an interest in veneering can start with some of the basic processes and move on to the use of more sophisticated tools and techniques as needed.

Figure 1-14. *Sidetable* by Jonathan Benson features fiddleback makoré, stained and bleached woods, curly maple, and a glass top. (30" x 30" x 18").

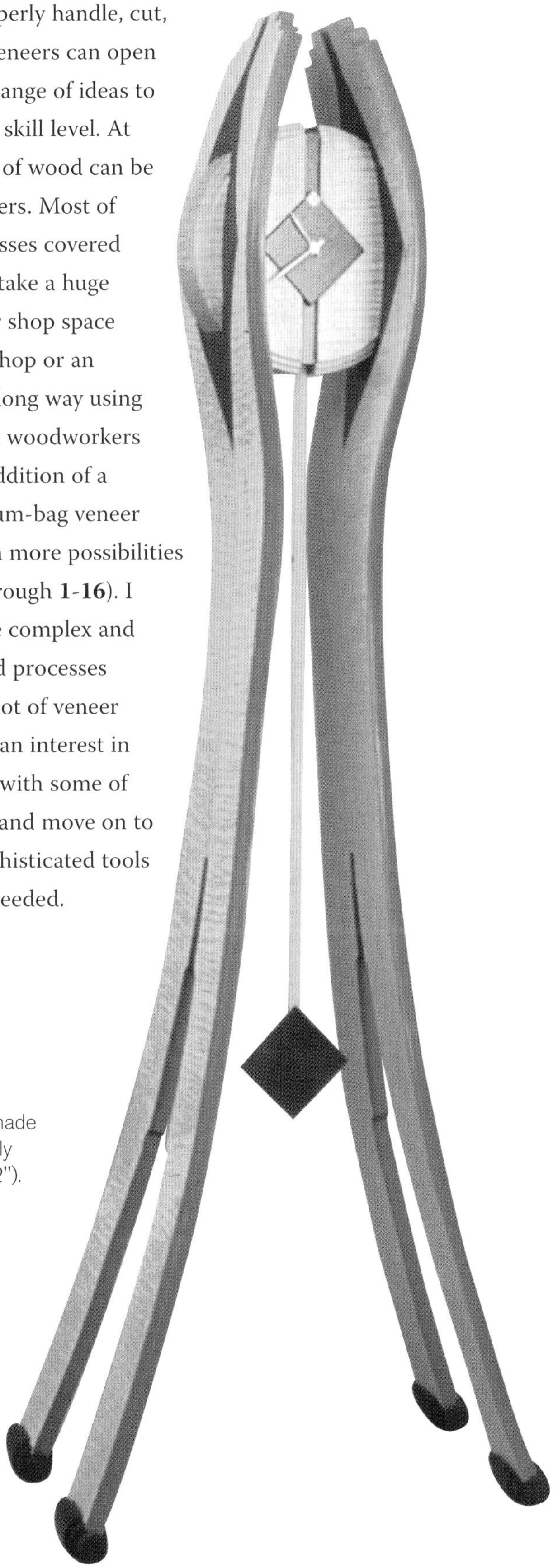

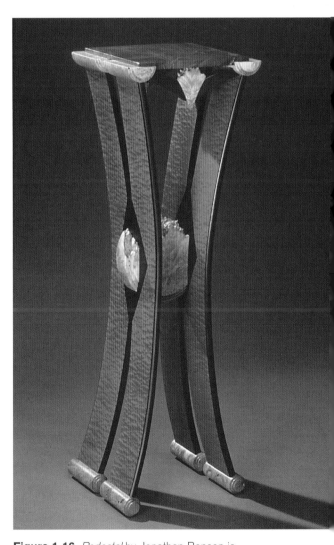

Figure 1-15. *Hands of Time* tall clock, by Jonathan Benson, is made of purpleheart and curly maple (62" x 26" x 12").

Figure 1-16. *Pedestal* by Jonathan Benson is made with pomele sapele veneer, maple burl, and a marble top (43" x 15" x 15").

CHAPTER 2

From Forest to Shop

Wood is an organic, dynamic material that continues to react to its environment long after it has been cut, dried, and finished. Knowing how and why woods react to moisture, seasonal changes, and sunlight is essential to creating effective designs that will last for generations.

Wood growth creates the grain patterns and figures seen on solid wood and veneers. Slicing veneers from a log creates the most beautiful wood out of the rarest, most interesting logs, and the process can produce a variety of figure patterns. An understanding of the manufacture of veneer helps the craftsman know what to expect when purchasing the material. Proper storage also is important to keep veneers flat, intact, and ready to use. The veneers shown in Chapter 2 are not enhanced by any wood finish—they are all raw wood, not sanded or finished.

Beautiful feather figure in black walnut arises where a large branch merges with the main trunk. The two leaves are book-matched.

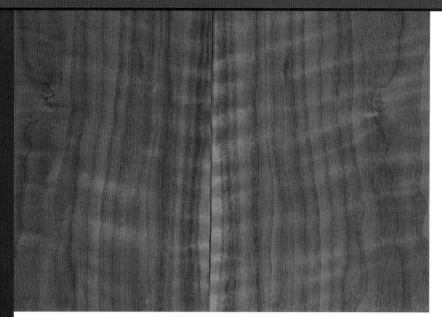

Figure 2-1. Many woods, such as these book-matched leaves of curly walnut, show light-colored sapwood alongside more deeply colored heartwood.

How wood grows

Wood grows by cell division: Cells divide outward to thicken and strengthen the tree's branches and trunk, and new branch and twig cells also grow upward to allow the tree to compete for sunlight. The growing cells accept and transport moisture and nutrients, much like a sponge absorbs water. As new cells are added, the older cells die and strengthen. The outermost layer of cells just under the bark, where the actual cell division or growth occurs, is referred to as the cambium layer.

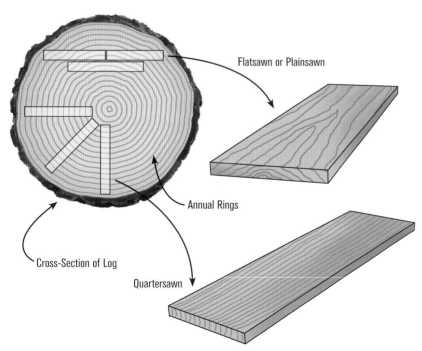

Flatsawn or Plainsawn

Annual Rings

Cross-Section of Log

Quartersawn

Figure 2-2. The way wood is sawn or sliced from the log determines the basic structure of its visible wood figure.

The dark-colored wood near the center of the trunk that ultimately supports the tree is known as the heartwood. Heartwood is most often used for woodworking. Sapwood, the layers of cells toward the outside of the trunk, transports sap, a mixture of moisture and nutrients, throughout the tree. Sapwood is often softer and lighter in color than heartwood, and is frequently discarded; however, particularly when matching veneers, the contrast in color between the heartwood and the sapwood can create a beautiful pattern to be used as a design element (**Figure 2-1**).

Wood cells are long, thin, and usually vertical. Individual cells cannot be seen by the naked eye, but long thin groups of cells known as fibers can be seen in most woods. The trunk grows outward during cell division, adding a new layer of wood each year. During the spring, a tree will grow relatively quickly, creating a layer of softer, lighter-colored wood. Then, in the summer and fall, growth slows, creating a denser, darker layer. The difference between the areas is seen as rings in the cross section of a tree (**Figure 2-2**), and cause what we see as the grain pattern in sawn boards. Different ways of sawing logs produce different grain patterns, as discussed on pages 20-21. Knowing how the cutting method affects grain pattern gives the craftsman a good idea of what to expect visually, a tremendous help in ordering and specifying wood and veneer.

Wood cells continue to absorb and give off moisture long after the tree has been sawn into boards or sliced into veneers. Summer's high humidity causes the cells to swell, while low humidity and indoor heating during winter cause the cells to shrink. This expansion and contraction occurs across the width and thickness of the cells or grain but rarely along the length, and movement is much greater across the rings than in between them. Wood finishes can slow, but not stop, this seasonal movement of wood. Using quartersawn lumber (see left), however, can greatly reduce wood movement.

Wood figure and wood movement

Figure refers to the visual patterns that appear on the surface of the wood (**Figure 2-3**). The patterns occur for a variety of reasons, including the wood fibers themselves, genetic mutation, disease, stress, or chance. Unusual figure sometimes appears when, for example, a crotch or feather pattern develops where two branches come together. Burls (**Figure 2-4**), cancerlike growths often caused by a wound or insect infestation, sometimes develop near the roots or on the trunk of a tree. When cut open, burls often have a complicated grain pattern

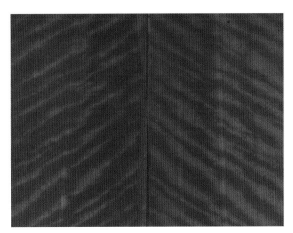

Figure 2-5. Fiddleback figure in makoré, a rare hardwood, resembles curl or fiddleback in American maple, though it is more richly colored. The book-matched samples here also show the reversal in light refraction from one side of the veneer leaf to the other.

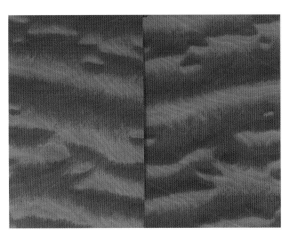

Figure 2-6. In quilted mouabi, the reflective whorls arise from the wood grain curving in and out of the surface. The two leaves here are book-matched.

Figure 2-3. Waterfall figure ripples across a sample of bubinga, a tropical hardwood from Africa. The unfinished sample is flat; the three-dimensional effect is due to light refraction.

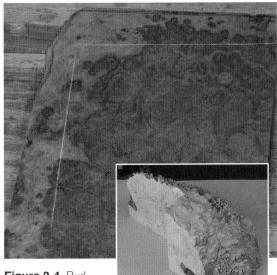

Figure 2-4. Burl veneer shows the irregular edge of its growth. The white lines indicate where it will be cut for figure matching.

Veneer TERMS

Clip, clipped. The process of straightening the long edges of veneer leaves is called clipping.

Flitch cut. Flitch cutting is slicing the veneer from a log along its length or from a slab (like peeling a carrot).

Flitch. A stack of veneer sheets sliced from the log and kept in sequential order, so the grain and figure match from one leaf to the next, is called a flitch.

Leaf, leaves. Sheets of veneer are also called leaves.

Rotary cut. Using a sharp knife to peel the veneer from a round log, similar to paper towels unrolling, is rotary cutting. The process is used mostly to manufacture plywood from crosswise layers of veneers and is used to cover large plywood and MDF panels with decorative veneers.

Wood grain, grain pattern. Long fibers that make up wood are the wood grain. Grain runs in the direction of the tree trunk, but it can also run toward a cut surface, "with the grain," or away from it, "against the grain." Grain is a factor in how wood appears.

Wood figure, figure pattern. The wood figure is the appearance of wood influenced by knots, straightness of the tree trunk, color changes between heartwood and sapwood, stains caused by minerals and chemicals in the wood, and marks made by weather, insects, or other trauma throughout the tree's life.

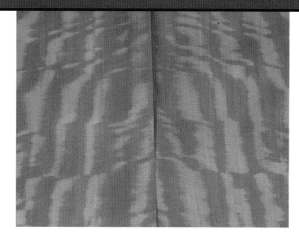

Figure 2-7. This African satinwood veneer shimmers due to the refractive properties of the wood grain.

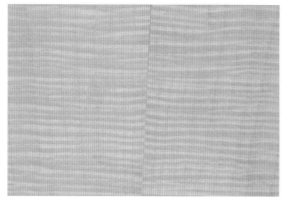

Figure 2-8. Curly, or fiddleback, maple veneer will show as lighter and darker bands when finished.

Figure 2-9. Pomele sapele shows many small blisters or bird's eyes in its figure. This sample is flat—the three-dimensional effect is entirely due to light refraction.

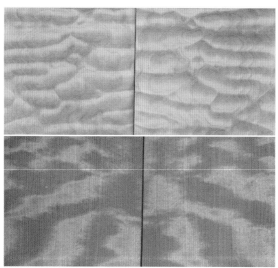

Figure 2-10. Quilted figure is also common in sapele and bigleaf maple.

that travels in all directions. Other processes, including genetic mutation, cause curl, swirl, blister, quilting, mottling, and bird's-eye patterns (**Figure 2-5** through **2-10**), but do not appear in all species of wood. Still another type of figure occurs when a tree has grown on a hillside or has partially toppled but continues to grow, creating compression of the grain on the underside of the trunk, and stretching of the grain on the upper side (**Figure 2-11**).

Highly figured woods are rare and valuable. In addition, particularly with the burls and such unusual figure as curl, bird's eyes, and quilting, the grain often has grown in many directions at the same time. The drying process and later seasonal expansion and contraction may cause the cut wood to split apart if not handled properly. One way to prevent splitting is to initially slice or saw these woods into thin veneers because veneers are inherently more stable than thicker solid wood.

Many design and construction situations do not allow for any wood movement. Methods to compensate for movement in solid wood construction are limited. Quarter-sawing lumber is one such method. Quartersawn wood moves less in width and more in thickness, but because the boards are relatively thin compared to their width, wood movement is less of a problem. Another solution to wood movement involves frame-and-panel construction. In this method, a panel is placed in a groove within a frame and allowed to float without being glued in place. Floating allows the panel to expand and contract across its width without affecting the overall dimensions of the frame. Veneer offers another approach to dealing with wood movement that allows for much more design flexibility. When thin veneers are securely glued to a stable surface (called a substrate), any movement across the grain is nearly eliminated. (For a complete discussion of substrates, please see Chapter 4).

Figure 2-11. The leaning trunk of this black cherry tree shows compression rippling, which will appear as curl in the wood cut from it.

How veneers are cut

Because veneers are such an efficient use of a limited material, the best logs usually are separated and sent to the veneer mill. There, they are stripped of bark and milled to the size and shape that best utilizes the particular characteristics of each log. The way of cutting the veneer from a log will yield different grain patterns and types of figure. The resulting grain or figure pattern for each type of cut also will vary according to the wood species. The basic methods for cutting veneer from a log are illustrated in the sidebar on pages 20 and 21. All methods use a large knife to slice the veneer from the unseasoned log.

Rotary Cutting

Rotary cutting involves placing the log between two centers, then rotating it against the knife. As the knife moves in at a set distance and pressure, the veneer peels off, much like paper unrolling. The grain pattern usually is quite uniform but cannot be book-matched. Rotary-cut veneer is used for the face of construction-grade plywood as well as the core material of some plywood. Rotary cut veneer covers large areas quickly, without the need for seams, and

is good for lower-cost surfaces that need a uniform appearance, such as doors, wall paneling, and plywood. Because there are few seams to telegraph through the paint, it also works well for surfaces that are to be painted. Bird's-eye maple is one of the few types of premium veneer cut this way. Rotary cutting maximizes the number and consistency of bird's eyes in each sheet.

Flitch Cutting

When sheets of veneer are sliced off the log (**Figure 2-12**) and kept together in sequential order, the resulting stack is known as a flitch (**Figure 2-13**). Veneer cut in this manner is referred to as flitch-cut veneer. Changing the orientation of the knife to the annual rings within the log creates a variety of grains and figures, which vary from species to species. Knowledge of wood characteristics is needed to best utilize each log. Veneer Slicing and Figure on pages 20-21 shows examples of common types of flitch cuts, and the resultant grain patterns and figures. To order veneer, the exact way the veneer is cut from the log is less important than knowing the types of grain and figure patterns available. Knowing the appearance of pattern and figure can create design possibilities and inspire new designs.

Figure in Veneer Species

Photos of veneers in my own inventory show examples of the color and figure available. Many of the species are not available as solid wood, and some, such as the pre-1992 vintage rosewood, are extremely rare. (Rosewood is protected; it is illegal to possess rosewood cut more recently than 1992). The samples have not been sanded or finished—what you see is the raw veneer. The examples are a fraction of the myriad of species and cuts available.

Beeswing andiroba

French ash burl

Mottled bubinga

Burl

Aromatic cedar

Cedar of Lebanon

Cocobolo, book-matched

Macassar ebony, book-matched

Macassar ebony, slip matched

Elm burl

Beeswing eucalyptus

Koa

Lovoa

Mahogany

Fiddleback makoré

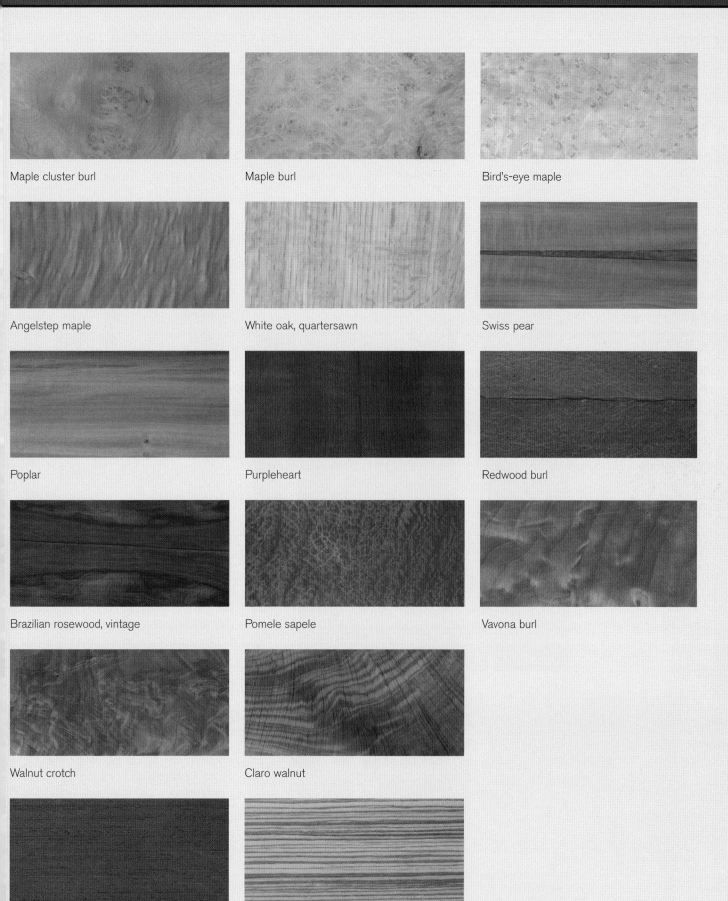

Maple cluster burl

Maple burl

Bird's-eye maple

Angelstep maple

White oak, quartersawn

Swiss pear

Poplar

Purpleheart

Redwood burl

Brazilian rosewood, vintage

Pomele sapele

Vavona burl

Walnut crotch

Claro walnut

Wenge

Zebrawood

After proper orientation of the log and knife are established, the log is cut to shape and conditioned by being boiled or steamed in large vats of water or chemicals. The conditioning softens the wood fibers, allowing them to be sliced cleanly without tearing, ripping, or splitting. An additional run of the log through the metal detector helps operators find and remove nails or other items that might damage the valuable, vulnerable knife edge. Veneers cut with a nicked knife exhibit either a raised mark or a trough running diagonally across each sheet (**Figure 2-14**). Veneers cut with a dull knife will have grain torn out on every other sheet. Both defects can add a lot of sanding time, particularly with harder woods, and should be avoided.

Figure 2-12.
A veneer-slicing machine moves the log against a heavy knife, which slices the veneer leaves. (Photo courtesy Erath Veneer Corporation.)

Figure 2-13. Flitch-cut veneers are carefully stacked in sequential order as they come off the slicing machine.

Clipping

Sheets of veneer are clipped, or cut straight along both long edges, to create sheets or leaves of uniform size with straight, uniform edges. Clipping usually removes the sapwood from each sheet.

Some wood species, and many burls, are available not clipped and have a rough or natural edge. With burls, which usually are odd-shaped before they are cut, the lack of clipping greatly reduces waste. Also, rough-edged veneers are good for capitalizing on the contrast between the sapwood and heartwood of a particular species because the sapwood has not been trimmed (**Figure 2-15**).

After clipping, veneer sheets are run though a dryer for specific times and temperatures, depending on thickness and species of wood. The sheets are then restacked in the order in which they came off the log and kept in a humidity-controlled environment until being shipped or used. Veneer sheets that require paper backing receive it at this point in the production process. Veneer without any factory backing or adhesive is known as "raw" veneer.

Buying veneers

After cutting and processing, the veneer is sent to a distributor. Large distributors cater mainly to large customers, providing rotary-cut sheets of veneer to plywood manufacturers for use as face veneer or paper-backed sheets of uniform, not unusual, quality to furniture and cabinet factories. Distributors are able to provide full flitches, which can number in the thousands of square feet. The rotary-cut sheets and paper-backed veneers are by no means bad. Large manufacturers of furniture, cabinets, and wall paneling want to be able to sell a consistent product nearly identical to the pieces they advertise, so color and figure uniformity is required. That requirement usually eliminates unusual grain patterns and figures from the veneered plywood and paper-backed veneer markets.

Medium and small distributors cater to smaller manufacturers and workshops looking for limited quantity, high-quality flitch-cut raw veneers. Most can provide anything from one sheet to an entire flitch (**Figure 2-16**), and there are hundreds of species available. Distributors and dealers can be found on the Internet. Most of these companies post photos of the veneer from the actual flitch you will be buying. In addition, there is an increasing number of businesses that sell veneer in joined, matched, and backed sheets, made of more unusual types of wood and grain patterns, for the high-end furniture and construction markets. Many of the distributors also sell tape, glue, and other veneering supplies.

Most distributors will send a small free sample upon request. Many sell sample packs containing 4" by 6" samples of twenty or thirty diverse woods, which are great to have around the shop for inspiration. I make sample boards of the most popular species by gluing a small piece of veneer to a thin substrate and then sanding and finishing it. Displaying the samples allows me to show clients what the finished product might look like. I also keep a fair amount of veneer inventory in my shop, so when I bid on a job I can make a sample board from the flitch of veneer I plan to use. I cut the sample in half, send the client one half, put their name on the back of the other half, and keep it, eliminating confusion later.

Flitch-cut, un-backed raw veneer is most often sold in lengths of 8' to 12' and known as full-length veneer, unless specified otherwise. Veneer also can be ordered in shorter lengths, which are referred to as shorts. Ordering veneer in an even number of sheets produces most matching patterns. Also, including an extra 15 to 20 percent more than you think you'll need is beneficial because ordering additional veneer a few weeks, or even a few days, later will probably mean the flitch originally ordered from is gone or the grain pattern has changed, and the veneer will not match.

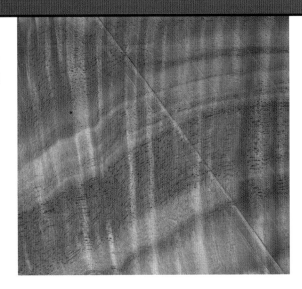

Figure 2-14. A nick in the slicing knife will leave a raised track across the face of the veneer.

Figure 2-15. These leaves of cocobolo have not been clipped—they retain the sapwood and the spreading shape of the tree trunk.

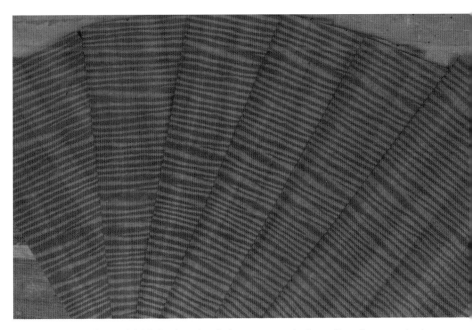

Figure 2-16. A flitch of fiddleback makoré shows a very similar pattern from one leaf to the next.

Veneer Slicing and Figure

The way the veneer mill slices the log affects the appearance of the veneer. The effect can be controlled by the orientation of the knife and log during the cutting process. There are two broad categories of veneer slicing: rotary and flat.

Rotary slicing

The log is placed between two centers and rotated while a wide, heavy knife is pressed into it, creating a long roll of veneer—much like paper unrolling. The figure repeats at intervals corresponding to the log's circumference. Rotary cutting can be centered, off-centered, or split.

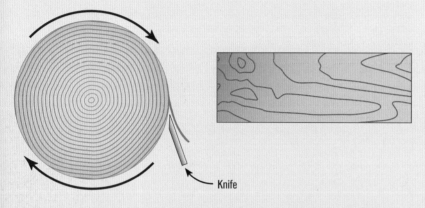

Knife

Rotary Slicing

Plywood is produced by rotary slicing. The process yields a continuous sheet of veneer with a consistent wavy grain pattern that generally repeats along the length. This method is very efficient and yields large sheets of veneer with a consistent grain pattern, but it does not necessarily create interesting figure and character.

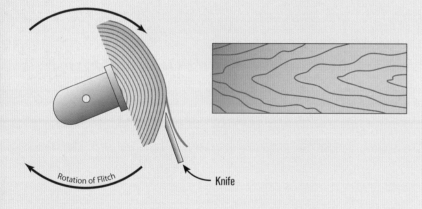

Rotation of Flitch

Knife

Half Round Slicing

In this method of slicing, the veneer closely follows the annual rings in the log. The result is wide, closely matched sheets with a wavy grain pattern. This veneer is good for covering large areas with a plain figure. This slice will also produce the most eyes in bird's-eye maple.

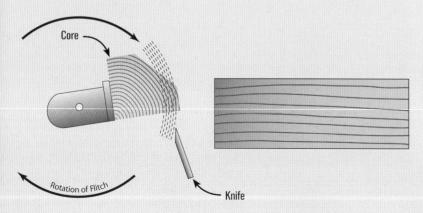

Core

Rotation of Flitch

Knife

Rift Slicing

This method can produce a linear grain pattern that closely resembles a common rift-sawn board. In some species rift slicing will emphasize the figure pattern known as mottling.

Flat Slicing

In flat slicing, the log is held stationary with respect to the knife, which advances into the log by the thickness of each successive leaf. Most veneer slicing machines have a stationary knife. A heavy apparatus grips the log, moving it up and down against the cutting edge. Flat-sliced veneers can be crown cut, quarter sliced, or quartered and then flat sliced.

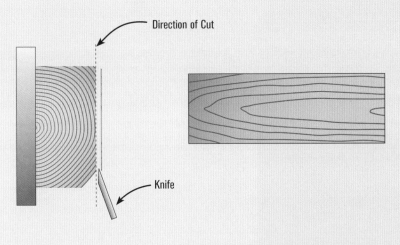

Plain Slicing (Flat Slicing)

Plain slicing is the most common method for producing flitch-cut veneers. It produces exactly matched consecutive sheets of veneer with a grain pattern resembling a flat-sawn board. The pattern will change slightly as the knife moves deeper into the log. If the edges are not clipped, some sheets will have uneven edges or will contain sapwood, which can be used to create interesting contrasts in color.

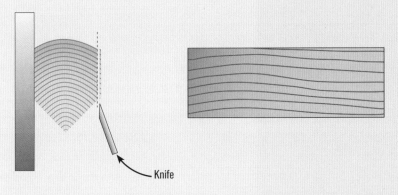

Quarter Slicing

Quarter-slicing will produce exactly matched quarter-sawn sheets with a strong linear pattern. It can also emphasize mottled figure in some woods. The quartered logs also can be rotated 90° to slice the veneer starting from the outside of the trunk, tangential to the curve of the annual rings. This will maximize the yield of quilted figure, which usually appears only near the surface of the log.

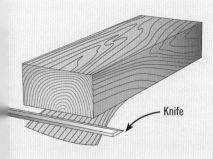

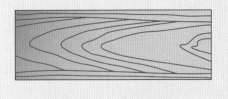

Lengthwise Slicing

Slicing lengthwise can produce a variety of grain patterns depending on the orientation of the log to the knife, the same as plain and quarter slicing. The difference is in the type of equipment. Lengthwise slicing is similar to the method you would use if you were to saw your own veneer, as detailed in Chapter 11.

Figure 2-17. Veneers should be stored on flat shelves. The author stores veneers high in his small workshop to save floor space.

Figure 2-18. Sheets of veneer should be numbered to keep them in order. (Use a white pencil on dark-colored veneers).

Storing veneers

Veneer usually arrives rolled tightly in a box. Rolling helps protect veneer during transit and shipping, but it should be stored flat. Most distributors store veneer in a humidity-controlled environment, which means it dries out when exposed to the normal atmosphere of the average shop. If the veneer is allowed to dry out when it is still rolled up, it will tend to hold that shape. Because veneer arrives while it is still slightly moist, it is easy to unroll without cracking and splitting. I store my veneer sheets on long shelves spaced 8" to 12" apart, high up and out of the way in my shop (**Figure 2-17**). The shelves are above the level of the doors and windows to prevent wind gusts from catching the veneer. A few cheap shelf brackets will hold the shelves up because they do not carry a lot of weight. The veneer usually comes wrapped in brown paper, which I place on top of each pile and between each species, to keep them clean, and, more importantly, away from sunlight to prevent fading. Scrap plywood on top of the stack of paper and veneer on each shelf further protects the veneer from any wind.

After unrolling the veneers, number the sheets in one corner with pencil or chalk (**Figure 2-18**). Numbering will allow you to create perfect matches later on, no matter how mixed up your sheets become. Number any time you acquire multiple sheets of veneer. If you plan on storing the veneer for any length of time, tape the ends across the width with veneer tape or high-quality masking tape the day it arrives, before it can dry out at all. Taping the ends prevents splits that otherwise could easily travel the entire length of a sheet (**Figure 2-19**).

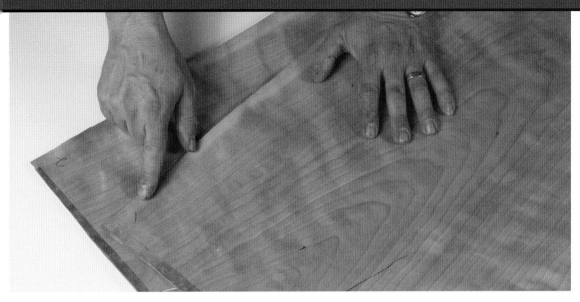

Figure 2-19. Tape the ends of veneers to protect them from splitting.

Check each sheet for defects (**Figure 2-20**). In addition to looking for lines from a chipped knife or tear out from a dull knife, see if each sheet is intact and in order. Sometimes improperly cut sheets can be hiding in the middle of a pile. Defects to look for include sheets that got folded over (a defect nearly impossible to fix), partial sheets, or sheets that are too thick or too thin in some areas. Also, closely examine the grain pattern, as out-of-order sheets could have been inserted into the stack, or the pattern could have changed over to another flitch. The defects rarely are attempts to cover mistakes by the manufacturer. The knife simply cuts so fast, and the process moves so much material at high speed, that close inspection of each sheet at every step is nearly impossible.

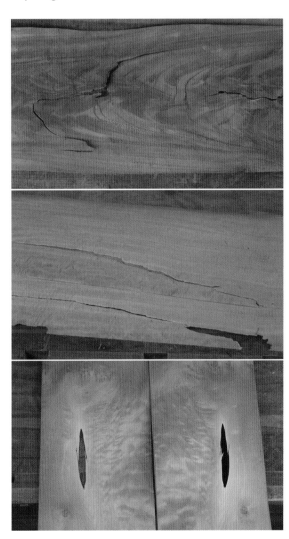

Figure 2-20. Common defects in veneers include cracks associated with knots, edge splits, and voids.

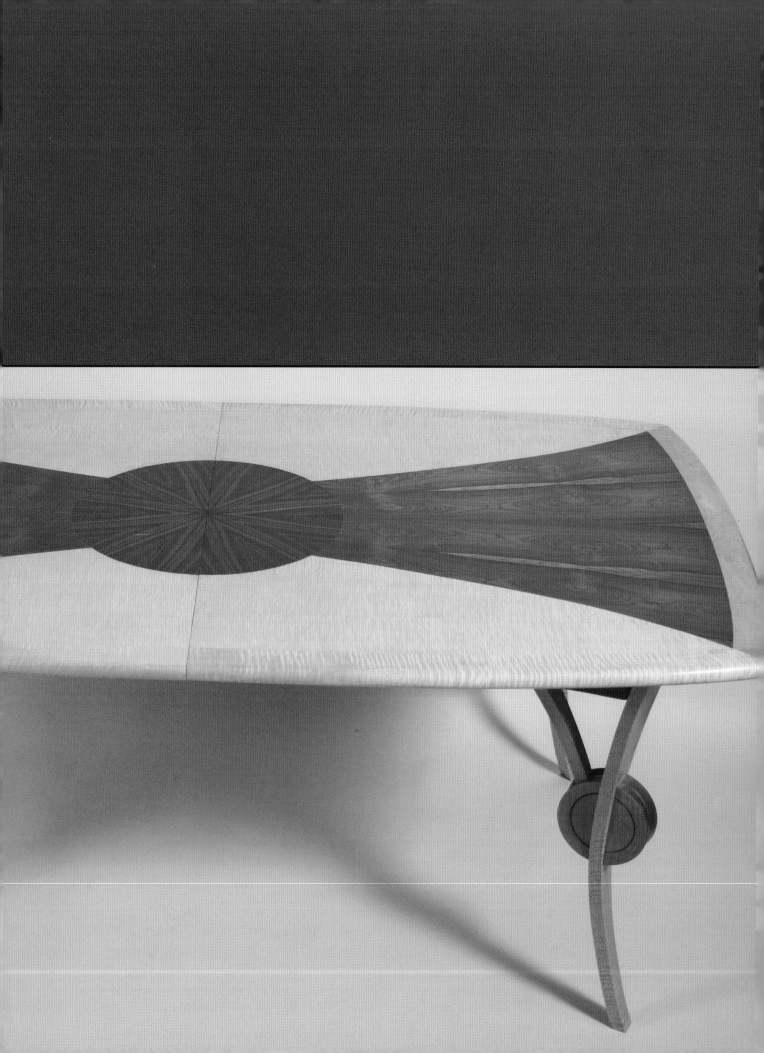

CHAPTER 3

Cutting, Matching & Taping Veneers

Rough cutting and laying up are the first steps in working with veneer. Laying up refers to the process of cutting, arranging, and taping the veneer into a single sheet ready to glue down on a substrate. Methods of arranging veneer fall into four basic categories: matching, parquetry, marquetry, and inlay. There are not always hard borders between these four categories, and many creative ideas come from combining them in new ways. My motto is, "If you can imagine it, you can make it."

These methods are demonstrated in this chapter and used to construct several projects throughout the book, beginning with a tabletop (**Figure 3-1**) that starts with the basic techniques and builds upon them. Demonstrated in the second part of this book (Chapter 12, page 140) is a mirror frame incorporating curved work. Much of the fun and enjoyment of using veneer, however, may be in finding new ways to work based upon a foundation of ideas, such as those presented in this book.

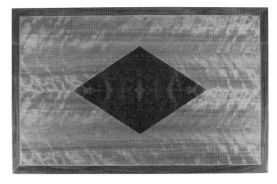

Figure 3-1. A veneered tabletop features a four-way burl match, inlaid into leaves of book-matched cherry, with a walnut border.

Dining Table by Jonathan Benson. The tabletop was made using the techniques presented in this book.

Figure 3-2. The back and sides of this 36" x 29" x 29" club chair, made by Pollaro Custom Furniture Inc. of Union, New Jersey, feature extravagantly book-matched burl veneers. (Photo courtesy Frank Pollaro.)

Four veneering styles

Matching, parquetry, marquetry, and inlay are the four basic approaches or styles in veneering. The first three differ in both intent and complexity—matched veneers, and/or parquetry, would be used to cover large surfaces and create a background for more intricate effects such as complex marquetry pictures. Any of these three styles may include inlaid lines and bands as well as small motifs or medallions.

Matching relies on sheets or leaves of veneer being kept in the order they are cut off the log, with each sheet looking nearly identical to the last. **Figure 3-2** shows an example of matched veneer. There are many variations of the process, which will be covered later.

Parquetry is the use of geometric patterns to create designs of contrasting woods or wood of a single species with contrasting figure or grain patterns (**Figure 3-3**). Often,

Figure 3-3. A veneered chessboard-under-construction is a good example of parquetry.

the contrasting grain and figure patterns create a three-dimensional effect.

Marquetry can be defined simply as pictures in wood (**Figure 3-4**). Methods for cutting the pieces for these pictures include using saws or sharp knives and chisels.

Inlay refers to veneer lines, bands, and small motifs set into a solid wood or veneered surface (**Figure 3-5**). Cabinetmakers often rout recesses for inlays in a glued-up surface. Veneer craftsmen generally cut and tape the inlay before it is glued down.

Veneer T E R M S

Book-match. Leaves of veneer joined so the front side of one sheet butts to the back of the next, like the pages of a book, are book-matched.

Inlay. A veneer motif, medallion, or band let into a precisely fitted recess cut into a larger veneered or solid-wood surface, with the surface finishing level, is an inlay.

Layup, laying up. A layup is assembly of veneer pieces fit neatly together and held in place by veneer tape.

Marquetry. Marquetry is the art of cutting and assembling small pieces of veneer into pictures.

Parquetry. The art of cutting and assembling small pieces of veneer into geometric patterns is parquetry.

Slip-match. Leaves of veneer joined so all the sheets are in order and facing the same side out, repeating the figure pattern across the panel, are slip-matched.

Substrate. The substrate is the base panel on which veneers may be glued. To avoid warping, the substrate must be veneered on both sides, not just one. Traditional substrates were made of solid wood, often sawn into narrow strips. Contemporary substrates most often are made of plywood or medium-density fiberboard.

Tape, taping. Taping describes the process of using veneer tape, a paper-based material, to hold pieces of veneer together in a layup. Most veneering projects require some amount of taping.

Figure 3-4. A school of veneer fish flows seamlessly around the curved perimeter of a pictorial marquetry desk (60" x 29" x 30") made by noted furniture artist Silas Kopf.

Figure 3-5. The light-colored maple band was inlaid into this veneered top before the laid-up top was glued to its substrate. The main field is vintage rosewood, with edging of Macassar ebony.

Matching veneers

Matching is the most basic and widely used method for arranging sheets of veneer. The most common types of matches, book matching and slip matching, rely on sheets or leaves of veneer cut from a log being kept in sequential order because each sheet closely resembles the next. In book matching (**Figure 3-6**), two sheets are opened up and placed next to each other like pages of a book. The figure patterns of the two sheets will mirror each other almost exactly, and the match can be continued by adding more sequential leaves from the veneer flitch. The process creates stunning designs that are not possible to duplicate by similar solid-wood boards.

When book-matching, a defect such as small knot or a variation in the wood grain can create unifying interest when repeated over a large area. When shopping for veneer, I always open up the flitch to see what type of matches can be created. A small mirror without a frame is a handy tool to see what a match may look like at different angles (**Figure 3-7**). For more complex matches, the mirror will become essential. Even when viewing veneer on the Internet, holding the mirror up to the screen can show what a sample match might look like. Many of the more complex patterns in this book are based on book-matching.

In slip-matching, instead of opening the sheets within a flitch like a book, the sheets are laid out next to each other in sequential order with the same side up, producing a repeated pattern (Figure 3-6). Slip-matching creates a uniform and pleasing design, a gentle unity that works in many applications. As the leaves are cut from deeper into the log, the figure pattern will start to change (**Figure 3-8**). Slip-matching minimizes changes, and may even allow for incorporation of sheets from other, similar flitches, which makes slip-matching ideal for large-scale projects. Plywood and MDF are manufactured with surfaces of either book-matched or slip-matched veneers; you must specify what type of match you want when ordering them.

Figure 3-6. The two leaves of Macassar ebony at right are book-matched, while the two at the left are slip-matched.

Figure 3-7. A small frameless mirror helps visualize the matches that are possible in a leaf of veneer.

Figure 3-8. The figure pattern slowly shifts as the veneer slicing progresses through the log.

Parquetry

A chessboard is the simplest form of parquetry. To make a chessboard, contrasting strips of veneer are cut into equal widths and taped together to make light-dark stripes (**Figure 3-9**). Then, the taped-up strips are cut perpendicular to their length at the same width as the original strips, and joined again (**Figure 3-10**). The process can be done using a variety of woods at any number of angles to create an almost infinite number of geometric patterns. A step-by-step demonstration sequence for making a checkerboard appears on page 131.

Parquetry using contrasting grain and satin-like woods can easily create the illusion of a three-dimensional surface, even with veneer of a single species. Some woods appear to be lighter or darker depending upon the angle from which they are viewed. For example, a piece of satinwood or some other wood with a satin-like appearance, rotated slowly, appears to lighten or darken as the light hits it from different angles. (See the Light Refraction sidebar on page 31.) Two pieces from the same board or sheet laid side by side with opposing grain directions will often appear darker or lighter than the other. When arranging veneer, flipping alternate pieces or turning around alternate sheets creates a three-dimensional effect. Although similar designs can be made with solid wood, seasonal wood movement would likely cause them to break apart eventually.

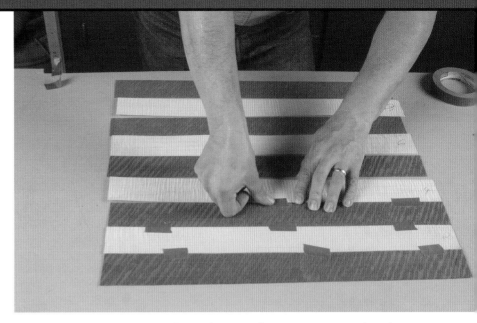

Figure 3-9. Parquetry begins with straight strips of contrasting veneers, here being taped up for a checkerboard.

Figure 3-10. Cutting the strips crosswise makes the checkerboard squares. Cutting at an angle would produce diamond shapes.

Marquetry

Marquetry covers several methods of creating pictures in wood. The oldest and most common is to use a fine saw to cut small, intricate pieces of wood and fit them together like a jigsaw puzzle. Once the picture has been assembled and taped into a single unit (**Figure 3-11**), it can be glued down as one piece on a suitable substrate (**Figure 3-12**). Another method is to place two pieces of veneer that will be next to each other in the design on top of each other, and then cut through both of them with a knife or saw. Doing so ensures both pieces will be the same shape, so they can fit together neatly. Often cutting techniques are combined. The knife is more suited to straight lines and simple curves, while the saw is more suited to sharp curves and small details. The sequence on pages 127-129 shows how to make a marquetry picture.

Cutting veneers

The first step in processing veneer is to rough cut it. Veneer always should be cut oversize and trimmed later. Rough cutting will eliminate many headaches and problems down the line. How much extra material is needed depends on two things: what type of edge the finished panel will have (refer to Chapter 7, page 76) and how many edges of each sheet are to be joined. The first cuts are oversize and do not need to be completely smooth—the key is to cut the veneer efficiently and without damage.

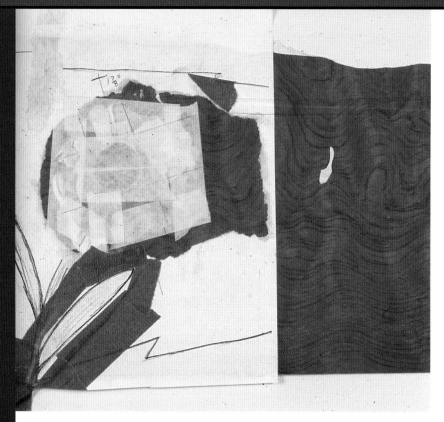

Figure 3-11. Small pieces of cut and sawn veneer are taped together before being glued onto a substrate.

Figure 3-12. This simple marquetry flower was pieced together from various veneers.

Light Refraction

When book-matching veneers, one leaf may appear darker than the other (**Figure 3-13**). Rotating the veneers or moving to the other side appears to reverse the effect. If the veneers are slip-matched with the same two faces up, the effect disappears. The difference in appearance is caused by light reflected from the wood to the eye at different angles, or refracted, depending on the surface of the wood. There are two basic reasons for the effect.

When veneer is cut from a log with a knife, each sheet will have a compressed, or tight, side and a pulled, or loose, side. On the compressed side, the wood fibers were pressed down under the pressure of the knife, while the fibers on the pulled side were stretched away from the surface above the knife as each sheet was peeled away. Examining a sheet of raw veneer closely shows one side usually has tiny grooves and grain tearout, and the fibers appear to be compressed. The other side, the pulled side, will have ridges, small lumps, raised grain, and sometimes tiny knife checks on the surface. The light will reflect back in different ways from these two sides even after sanding. If the veneer is slip matched, this will not be noticeable. If the veneer is book-matched, allowing a view of the compressed side and pulled side at the same time, one side may appear darker.

The additional cause of different light refraction from two sides of the same sheet of veneer lies in the wood structure. Woods with a lot of figure, such as quilting or curl, and those with a satin sheen, contain grain fibers that travel not only along the length of the wood, but also up, down, and even sideways. When these wood fibers are sheared off, a figured grain pattern appears. Wood fibers that leave the veneer surface at different angles will reflect light back at different angles. In addition, light refraction can intensify figure in many types of woods, or cause a three-dimensional appearance. The refractory quality can easily be seen in quilted maple (Figure 3-13) and in quilted mouabi (**Figure 3-14**). Notice how the quilts in the photo appear to rise up from the surface and form convex billows—in actuality, these veneers are quite flat. To make the book-match, one sheet was flipped over, making the quilt shapes appear to be concave hollows. Satinwood and woods with a satinlike quality have traditionally been used to create geometric parquetry patterns in this way. A herringbone pattern can also emphasize this quality of wood grain.

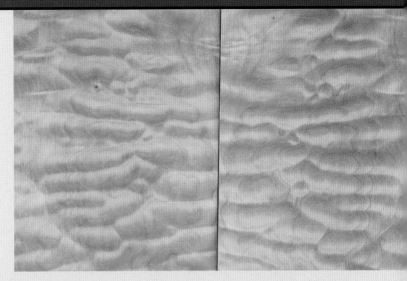

Figure 3-13. Woods such as satinwood and quilted maple reflect light differently, according to the angle at which they are viewed.

Figure 3-14. The refractory effect in quilted mouabi can be used to create shimmering parquetry patterns.

Crosscutting Veneers to Length

In most cases, the veneer is crosscut first, usually with a veneer saw (sometimes called a veneer knife) (**Figure 3-15**), guided by a straight board. A board clamped down over the veneer pile on the side of the veneer that will be kept (as shown in the Step-by-Step procedure on page 33) helps in several ways. The board keeps the veneer from sliding around, binding, and splitting from the movement of the saw. It also keeps the cut in exactly the same place on each sheet, which greatly aids in measuring and matching later.

The most common problem is tearout of the veneer as the saw runs through the sheet at the edges. The best solution for this is to always cut toward the center from the edge. Push the saw away from you when cutting the closest side of the veneer and pull the saw toward you when cutting the far side. Saw in one or two inches from both edges, and then cut the center. Cut through the edges of several layers at once. Then, cut through the center of one sheet at a time. After each sheet has been sawn through, pull the waste away from the cut to avoid getting it caught up in the saw.

Other methods of crosscutting work well, too. A paper cutter, the type with a large arm to pull down over the material to make a cut, does a good job on one sheet at a time. Be careful, though, because some species of wood may tear more than they cut and are not suited for cutting in this way. However, the paper cutter is a great tool for fine-trimming small pieces in

Figure 3-15. A Japanese veneer saw is shown at top, with a Western-style saw at bottom.

Figure 3-16. Stout utility scissors can crosscut many veneers.

Figure 3-17. Sacrificial boards taped to the veneer stack keeps the table saw from splintering the wood. The crosscut box is a big help when sawing veneers and veneered panels. You can prevent any movement during sawing if you nail the stack to the crosscut box. Nail through an area that will be waste.

detail work and also for cutting paper-backed veneers. A stout pair of scissors or utility snips (**Figure 3-16**) also works well enough on most veneers. In fact, the scissors work very well on paper-backed veneers because the paper keeps the veneer from splitting.

Veneer sheets can be crosscut with a chop or table saw, using a blade that has as many teeth as possible. To prevent the veneer from tearing apart, sandwich it tightly between sacrificial scrap boards (sacrificial because they are sawn right through with the veneer) (**Figure 3-17**).

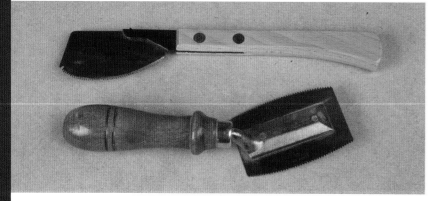

Crosscutting veneers to length is a fundamental technique needed in every veneering project.
The objective is to make a clean, straight cut in the same place on many sheets or leaves.

Step 1. Stack the veneers and draw a layout line to be sawn.

Step 2. Clamp a straight guide board or fence along the line to be sawn.

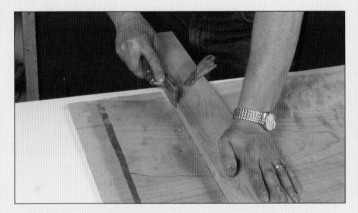

Step 3. Saw in from the edge nearest you, several sheets at a time.

Step 4. Saw in from the far edge. Keep the saw tight against the guide board.

Step 5. Saw the center of the stack one sheet at a time.

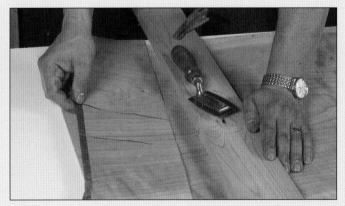

Step 6. Pull the cut pieces away from the saw to keep them away from subsequent cuts.

Ripping Veneers to Width

After crosscutting to rough length, the veneer must be rough-cut along its length. A veneer saw works best because a knife tends to follow the grain away from the intended cut line. Just as when crosscutting, the sheets are sawn a little oversize. I usually saw the edges that are to be joined about ⅟₁₆" to ⅛" wider than the finished width. I use a wood straightedge as a guide (**Figure 3-18**) because a metal straightedge would dull the saw. Also, the saw will wear down any metal straightedge, making it useless for creating a straight line ever again.

The cut is not the final seam, so it can be a little rough. Even so, it will pay off to take the time to tape the veneer stack tightly together at the ends (**Figure 3-19**). The taped stack will closely resemble the board, with the grain on all four edges flowing through, just as it did before being sliced into veneer, making every cut fall on exactly the same spot relative to the figure pattern on each sheet. Even if a little more or less is cut off than intended, there will still be an automatic, perfect match every time. Pulling away the drop-cut sheets prevents them from getting caught up in the saw (**Figure 3-20**). If the sheets in the stack are to be used later, they should be numbered for matching. After sawing, the stack should remain taped together.

Choose A or B

When laying out matched veneers, it is necessary to keep track of which side will be the show surface and which will be glued down. Some people only mark the bottom. I prefer to mark an A on all the tops and a B on all the bottoms. Use pencil on light-colored woods and white pencil on dark-colored ones.

If you are making panels that match each other, lefts and rights, you may need to switch the A and B sides. Do this after you have taped up each panel.

Figure 3-18. Rip the veneer sheets to width using a guide board and a veneer saw. The guide board can be clamped or hand-held on the good side of the line.

Figure 3-19. Before sawing, tape the veneer stack together at the ends so the individual leaves can't slide around.

Figure 3-20. Saw through one leaf at a time and remove the waste strip before continuing to saw.

Shooting the edges

After crosscutting and ripping the veneers to rough size, the next step is creating a seamless joint between each sheet, a process known as shooting. Shooting a straight, square, and clean edge is essential. Otherwise, there will be ugly gaps in the finished surface. The various jigs and fixtures used to create seamless joints are called veneer shooters. A shooter is intended to create a long joint with no gaps. In almost all of the methods for shooting veneers, the veneer is stacked so that many edges can be cut true and straight at once. I usually use a combination of methods during a veneer project. Methods may be altered, combined, or developed to suit your particular needs.

Jointer Plane

The traditional method to shoot edges is to clamp the veneer sheets between two straight boards, and use a long jointer plane to straighten and square the veneer edges as if they were a solid board (**Figures 3-21** and **3-22**). A good straightedge can be used during this process to check how straight the edges are.

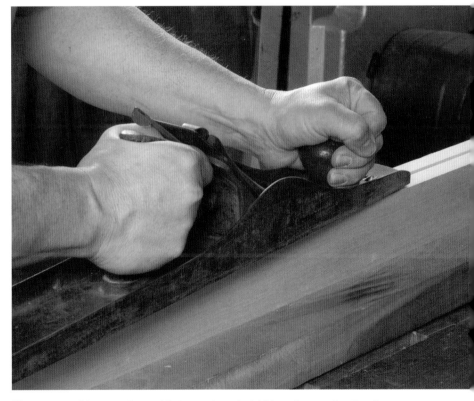

Figure 3-22. Veneers clamped between two straight boards or a shooting jig can be shot with a jointer plane.

Jointer

The method I prefer uses a shooting jig that is run over the jointer. As shown in **Figure 3-23** and **3-23A**, the jig consists of two ¾"-thick straight, flat boards of poplar or some other good medium-quality wood. Two thicker boards or cauls to help reinforce the structure, and two bolts with wing nuts permit easy loading and unloading of the veneer. The veneer sheets are placed in the jig in a stack with ⅟₁₆" to ⅛" of extra width exposed beyond the edge of the jig (**Figure 3-24**). A few scraps of veneer or a scrap of ⅛" plywood is placed in the center of the jig to keep pressure on the center. The thicker center boards also could be bowed toward the middle to create even pressure along the length of the jig. After the wing nuts are securely fastened, the whole jig

Figure 3-23. The jointer shooting jig consists of two straight boards, each stiffened by an attached caul, with the veneers sandwiched in between. Bolts and wing nuts tighten the jig on the veneers.

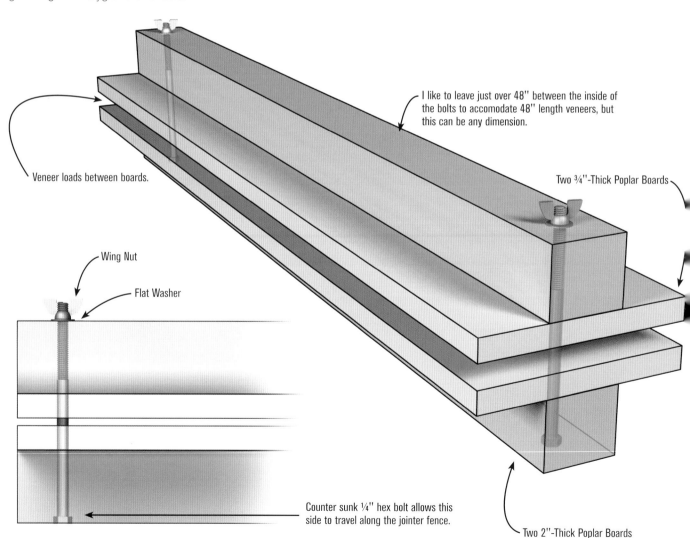

I like to leave just over 48" between the inside of the bolts to accomodate 48" length veneers, but this can be any dimension.

Veneer loads between boards.

Two ¾"-Thick Poplar Boards

Wing Nut

Flat Washer

Counter sunk ¼" hex bolt allows this side to travel along the jointer fence.

Two 2"-Thick Poplar Boards

Figure 23A. Jointer shooter.

Figure 3-24. Adjust the veneers so ¹⁄₁₆" to ⅛" protrudes from the jig.

Figure 3-25. The jointer fence guides the shooting jig. Please note: The guard was removed to show the cuts. Do not remove the guard from your tool.

is run over the jointer (**Figure 3-25**). Each use shaves a little bit off the thinner boards. Even so, I have found it takes several years before they need to be replaced. If the jointer is properly tuned, the method described is the fastest and most accurate way to shoot veneer. It is also safe if you leave the guard on the jointer.

To avoid tearout, make sure the jointer knives are sharp and pass the jig over the jointer very slowly. The grain direction of the veneer relative to the jointer can also be reversed by turning it around.

Sanding Stick

Some veneers either have too much variation in grain or are too brittle to pass over the jointer at all. In such cases, I cut the waste veneer down to ¹⁄₁₆" or less from the edge of the jig and then bring it flush with the jig using a sanding stick (**Figure 3-26**). A sanding stick is an approximately 1"-wide strip of wood with sandpaper glued to it using contact cement. I have several grits available because harder, denser woods require coarser grits to sand than do softer woods. If the center of the shooting jig becomes bowed due to sanding, run the empty jig over the jointer to straighten it.

The process of using the sanding stick and some type of shooting board is invaluable when matching small pieces of veneer for complex projects. If veneers such as burls are too brittle or wrinkled to work with, they can be flattened and moistened by sizing them, following the procedures for sizing detailed in Chapter 8.

Figure 3-26. The sanding stick makes short work of shooting brittle veneers, which are held in a shooting jig.

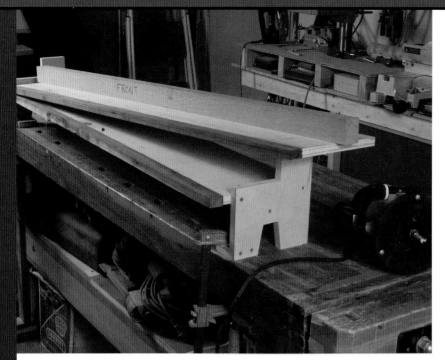

Figure 3-27. The router shooting jig has two parts, a top plate and a bed plate, both with thick straight cauls. The end frames, which have ears for clamping to the workbench, hold the jig parts in place.

Router

Another method for shooting veneer is to use a router jig similar to the one in **Figures** 3-27 and 3-28. The jig can take many forms, but most are similar to the one shown. As usual, the sheets of veneer are secured between two boards, with a thicker board slightly bowed in the center to ensure even pressure along the length of the veneers, or a clamp is placed in the center for additional pressure (**Figure 3-29**). A sharp flush-trim bit is placed in the router. I prefer to use a bit with four cutters to get a smoother cut. The bit rides on the edge of the jig (**Figure 3-30**), so it is critical to use straight boards when constructing this jig. If the veneer begins to tear out, the router can be run in the opposite direction. This jig also can be used with a sanding stick.

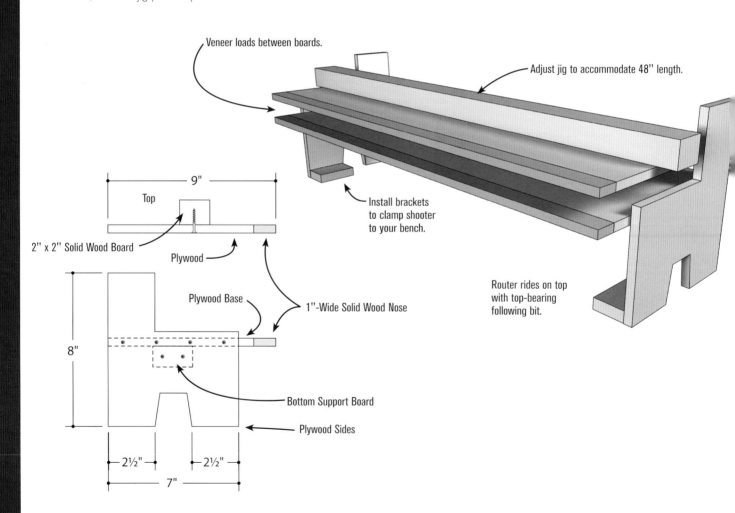

Figure 3-27A. Router shooter.

Figure 3-28. Clamp the jig onto the veneers and to the workbench, and guide the router along its straight edge.

Figure 3-29. To increase the center pressure in the jig, insert a few leaves of veneer.

Figure 3-30. The router bit has a ball bearing on top of its cutting flutes, which guides it along the edge of the shooting jig.

Figure 3-31. A down-spiral router bit gives the best results on brittle veneers, but it has no bearing, so the router must be guided by a rail on the jig.

There are several variations of the jig. Some have the router running against a fence, allowing for the use of a downward spiral-cutting bit like the one shown in **Figure 3-31**. That reduces tearout, even when shooting very brittle veneers. The two jigs are quite similar, so it is a matter of personal preference as to which is best suited to your particular needs and equipment.

Table Saw

Sandwich-type shooting jigs can be made to pass over the table saw. The jigs consist of an upper and a lower board with the veneer secured between them; another variation has a strip of wood that rides in the slot of the table saw. These types of sandwich jigs rarely leave the veneer edge smooth enough for finished joining and taping. However, the type of sandwich jig in **Figure 3-32** does a fine job if everything is nailed down tightly. The other sandwich jigs don't apply enough pressure when the veneer is being cut.

Figure 3-32. Sandwich the veneers between two pieces of MDF and cut them using the table saw crosscut sled.

Figure 3-33. To shoot with a sharp knife, clamp a metal straightedge to the work and apply center pressure by inserting a few scrap veneers there.

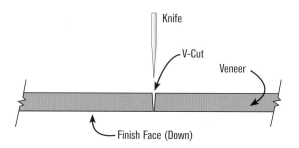

Figure 3-34. The finest knife still makes a V-shaped cut in the veneer.

Knife and Straightedge

Shooting with a knife and straightedge works well for small pieces of veneer, one or two pieces at a time, and is essentially the same as knife-cutting an inlay into a veneer field (**Figure 3-33**). The method works on soft and straight-grained woods and many paper-backed veneers. A metal straightedge works best here and needs to be securely fastened down. As noted before, sometimes the knife follows the wood grain away from the intended cut. One solution is to purchase a special veneer knife that stays against the straight edge and is easy to grasp.

The knife-cut method gets harder the longer you make the cut. The seam often becomes uneven, and gaps start to develop along an extended length. A breakaway knife works well when cutting small pieces for detail work. A

utility knife will work, but it makes a thicker cut, causing difficulty when fitting the veneer pieces together later on. Any knife will make a V-shaped cut, which creates a gap on one side of the veneer (**Figure 3-34**). Always insert the knife from the bottom of the veneer. Doing so allows for a tight fit on the A side, or top side, with any gaps hidden underneath on the B side. Knife-cutting techniques, such as inlaying and creating curved joints, are described in detail in Chapter 9.

Veneer Saw

The final shooting method is to use a veneer saw and a straight edge. You can shoot several sheets of veneer at the same time, using the same set up and veneer saw method described on page 34 for rough-ripping veneers to make a finish cut. To make a finish cut, the saw needs to be sharp, the straight edge needs to be exactly straight, and everything needs to be tightly secured. Veneer saws can be sharpened easily (**Figures 3-35** to **3-37**).

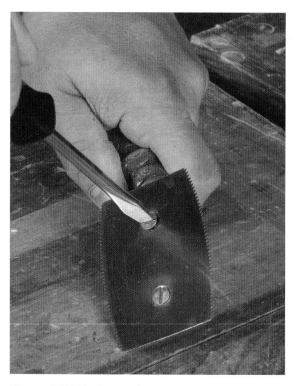

Figure 3-35. To sharpen the veneer saw, remove the blade from the saw handle.

Figure 3-36. Clamp the saw blade between two pieces of wood, and file the teeth with a small triangular file.

Figure 3-37. Use the side of a sharpening stone to remove any burr or set from the saw teeth.

A variation of the method is to shoot the veneer in two steps. First, use the straightedge and saw to cut the veneer close to size, leaving about ¹⁄₁₆" to the intended finish line. Next, shift the veneer under the straightedge to bring the final cut line right up to the edge. Then, use a sanding stick or hand plane to bring the veneer flush with the straightedge.

Taping

After crosscutting, ripping, and shooting, the next step is to tape the veneer sheets together. There are two objectives—to pull all of the joints tight and neat, with all of the veneer pieces held securely in place; and to end up with all the tape on the top, or A side, leaving the back, or B side, clean and clear for gluing.

Refer to the sidebar on tapes (see page 42) for selecting the proper tape. The veneer is taped first on the B side with blue painter's tape (**Figure 3-38**). Then, the whole taped-up sheet is flipped over so the A side can be taped with paper veneer tape, which is relatively easy to remove after gluing and pressing (**Figure 3-39**). Finally, blue painter's tape must be removed from the B side before gluing. Any blue painter's tape left on the B side will cause a bubble in the glued-up panel.

Figure 3-38. Tape the back side of the veneer, the side that will be glued down, with blue painter's tape.

Figure 3-39. On the top or show side of the veneers, tape across the seams with short lengths of paper veneer tape. Three-hole tape helps you see how the seam is lining up.

Choosing Tape

Several types of tape can be used in the process of veneering: regular masking tape, blue painter's masking tape, and several varieties of paper veneer tape (**Figure 3-42**). The basic strategy is: Pre-tape everything with blue painter's tape on the B side. Tape the A side with veneer tape. Remove the blue painter's tape before gluing. The strategy provides the advantage of the quick adhesion of blue painter's tape while fitting veneer pieces together and the ease of removal of the veneer tape after the panel has been glued up.

Figure 3-42. Use blue painter's tape for the back side of veneer layups because it is easy to remove and leaves no residue. Use paper veneer tape for the top or show surface. Paper veneer tape comes in full, two-hole, and three-hole varieties, offering different amounts of visibility through the holes.

Blue painter's tape can be removed easily and put back when refining details of a project, even after it has been on veneer for a few days, and leaves no residue to interfere with gluing. Regular masking tape, which some craftsmen prefer, tends to pull the veneer apart when it is removed, particularly if it has been left on for more than a day or two. Masking tape usually leaves a residue. Masking tape should never be left on the veneer when gluing up under pressure because it becomes embedded and is virtually impossible to remove without destroying the veneer.

Veneer tapes come in several types, including solid, two-hole, and three-hole. The solid is strongest, easiest to use, and good for long, straight seams in even-grained woods. The two- and three-hole veneer tapes are not as strong as solid tape, but can be seen through somewhat during complicated procedures.

Solid veneer tape or blue painter's tape should never be left on the underside of the veneer during the gluing process. The veneer will not adhere in those areas, and bubbles will inevitably result. Three-hole tape can be used when for some reason, such as when making some bent laminations, tape must remain on the underside of the veneer. The veneer will come into contact with its substrate through each hole in the tape, which is enough to hold most veneers. Contact will occur work with tape that has a maximum number of holes.

Veneer tape must be moistened, and several types of applicators are available. I usually use a damp kitchen sponge in a bowl with a little water (**Figure 3-40**). Once the tape has been applied, I iron it down quickly with a common iron set on warm, not hot (**Figure 3-41**). The heat creates an instant bond.

At this point, I transfer all numbers back to the A side in case I need to know lefts, rights, tops, and bottoms. Once any project is laid up, I always place the taped sheets between two pieces of plywood to keep them safe and flat. One false move can destroy many hours of work and much veneer.

Figure 3-40. Wet the tape and press it down on the veneer seams. Run the long tape right over the short cross-pieces.

Figure 3-41. Veneer tape may be ironed to dry and set the adhesive.

As noted in the introduction to Chapter 3, I'm demonstrating a rectangular tabletop project with a burl inlay and will continue to work on it as the book progresses. This section involves making a book-matched background field of cherry veneer. How you mark the veneers is important because the marks will be relied on in subsequent steps. Remember to use pencil on light wood and white pencil on dark wood.

Taping the veneers into a stack will help shoot the edges. If the design has more than two sheets, there will be a joint on both edges of each leaf and the stack will need to be shot on both edges. Be certain the interior sheets have enough extra width to allow for shooting on both edges. Remember, because two sides of a joint are being cut with each pass, you are actually removing double the width you are cutting off. For example, if 1/16" is exposed beyond the edge of the shooter, 1/8" is being removed from the width of the finished panel. Make each sheet just a little wider than the original design, even if it means the two outer sheets of your panel end up a little narrower than the rest.

Shooting clean and straight edges is critically important. A seam that has a gap in it cannot be pulled together with tape and stay together when the whole sheet is glued down. The seams must be perfectly tight.

Step 1. Open the veneers, align them for the best figure match, and then trim them to rough size. Number them. Mark which sides will be A sides, or tops, and which will be B sides, or bottoms.

Step 2. Stack the veneer sheets together, taping them on the ends to create a board similar to the one from which they were sliced into veneers. Load the taped stack into the shooting jig and shoot one edge. Then, remove the two outer leaves and retape the stack to shoot the opposite edges.

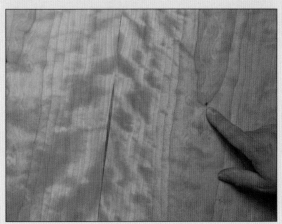

Step 3. After shooting the edges, lay the leaves out side-by-side to make sure the seams are tight and the match is what you want. If the seams are not perfect, restack the veneers, retape the ends, and shoot again. When the process is completed, tape the seams using paper veneer tape.

CHAPTER 4

Substrates

A substrate is the surface to which veneer is attached. A veneer surface can be only as good as its foundation. For centuries, the most common veneering substrate was solid wood, which has the problem of wood movement and consequent damage to the surface veneers. Other substrates developed primarily to solve the problems of solid wood include plywood, particleboard, MDF, and lumber core.

Veneered furniture often incorporates curved panels, making bendable substrates necessary. Bendable substrates include laminated panels made up of many thin layers of wood, bending plywood, and Kerfcore. Weight also is a problem because MDF, which is otherwise excellent for substrates, is dense and heavy. Lightweight substrates include shop-made torsion boxes and honeycomb sheets.

Walnut veneer is laid on a solid wood substrate in this panel.

Substrate selection criteria

Consider a few basic principles to help select the best material for a substrate.

- The substrate material must have a structural integrity of its own. A layer or two of veneer will not strengthen a weak substrate.
- The surface can only be as good as what lies beneath it. The substrate must be free of face defects because they may telegraph through to the applied surface veneer.
- The core must be free of delaminations and internal defects that could cause the panel to separate.
- The surface must be able to bond well with the veneer.

Other considerations include the substrate's ability to bend if necessary, its weight, and its cost. Different substrates might be combined within a given project to capitalize on the strengths of each.

When possible, I make veneered panels oversize and trim them later, which allows for any slipping and sliding during the gluing process. I wait to trim the panel until the last minute, which keeps the edge protected for as long as possible. I even do most of the scraping and sanding of the surface before I trim the panel to final size, just to provide extra protection to those delicate edges.

Substrate T E R M S

Crossband. Veneer laid under the face veneer and at right angles to it, to stabilize the panel and improve the adhesion of the face veneers to the substrate or ground, is called crossband veneer or counter-veneer.

Cross-grain lamination. Cross-grain lamination is made up of thin layers of wood, with their grain direction running at 90 degrees from layer to layer.

Lamination, laminate, delaminate. Layers of wood glued together are called laminae or laminates. The assembled panel is called a lamination. If the layers should become unglued and separate, they are said to have delaminated.

Medium-Density Fiberboard. Medium-density fiberboard, or MDF, is a man-made material composed of wood chips and glue, with a uniform texture and a firm surface layer. MDF is an ideal substrate for veneer.

Particleboard. A man-made material consisting of coarser particles than MDF, particleboard is usually not suitable for veneering.

Plywood. Hardwood plywood is a man-made material consisting of many thin layers or laminations of wood glued together, with the grain in the wood running crosswise from layer to layer. Plywood is a good substrate for veneer. Most plywood has an odd number of layers.

Traditional substrates

Veneered tops on solid wood surfaces often are crossbanded with another layer of veneer (**Figure 4-1**). Crossbanding refers to laying down two sheets of veneer in opposing grain directions to help lock them in place, preventing the top layer from moving back and forth across its grain. The grain direction of the bottom veneer is sometimes laid perpendicular to the grain of the substrate in an effort to prevent wood movement. At other times, the veneer is laid with the same grain direction as the substrate to allow both to move at the same time. Unfortunately, in both cases, the solid wood substrate continues to expand and contract with changes in atmospheric humidity, causing either the top to bow, cup, and twist, or the veneer to crack and split. The movement from underneath also could cause the veneer to come unglued. I have reglued the veneer for many such antique pieces in my shop.

Another type of substrate incorporates the idea of cross-grain lamination, in which thin sheets of wood are stacked with opposing grain directions to lock them in place, preventing seasonal movement. Although it is essentially the same as modern plywood, the method for creating a stable substrate for veneering originated in ancient Egypt. The process was mostly lost, however, until the industrial revolution of the nineteenth century. A patent for plywood was first given to John Mayo, an American, in 1865. Plywood came into wide use in the early twentieth century with the development of synthetic glues and the hydraulic hot press. Substrates incorporating this principle, which are either manufactured by industry or shop-made, remain an excellent option for a base for veneering.

One issue common to most veneered work is how to manage the edge of the substrate. The simplest answer is to cover the edge with a veneer or with a thin strip of solid wood (**Figure 4-2**).

Figure 4-1. The front corner of a walnut-veneered panel shows the crossbanding between the face veneer and the substrate.

Figure 4-2. The solid wood edging, or lipping, on this panel was applied before the veneer was glued down. The face veneer covers the lipping. If the edging had been applied after the face veneer, a line would be seen where the two joined.

Plywood substrates

The important principle to consider is that, when constructing plywood or adding veneer to a surface, the grain of each layer must always alternate. If the grain direction of the outer layer is in the same direction as the layer below it, the outer layer will crack, bubble and separate. If too many layers of veneer in a substrate have grain that travels in the same direction or if the top and bottom face of a panel have opposing grain directions, the panel will bow. To achieve stability, there should be an odd number of layers or plies, the grain direction should alternate from layer to layer, and the surface veneer should be laid cross-grain to the substrate's top layer.

Figure 4-3. The grain direction alternates from layer to layer in these plywood substrates. In general, the more layers in the plywood, the better for veneering.

Figure 4-4. Construction-grade plywood, as well as construction materials such as OSB (bottom), is unsuitable for veneer work. Their rough surfaces, cracks, and voids would likely telegraph through the veneered surface.

Occasionally, in a bent panel, for example, you may need an even number of layers. In that case, make the two layers that have the same grain direction the center layers. By doing so, the tension will be equal on both sides of the panel.

When selecting manufactured plywood as a substrate, use only the best grade available. Cabinet-grade plywood of birch, poplar, and lauan are good substrates for most veneering projects (**Figure 4-3**). The three materials are stable for two reasons. First, all of the layers, including the face, are made from stable species of woods that contain few imperfections. Some still have a softwood core, while others have a core consisting of the same species as the surface veneer, which I strongly recommend. Second, compared to construction-grade plywood, cabinet-grade plywood often contains more layers. Generally, the more layers a panel contains, the thinner the layers will be, and the more stable it will be. Plywood is sold with a varying number of layers within a particular thickness. For example, ¾" plywood is available in some species containing five plies, seven plies, or as many as 13 plies. The thinner layers tend to move less, and there is more glue surface to hold each layer in place.

Many options are available. Baltic birch is one of the higher quality substrates. As with most species of woods used in the manufacture of plywood, the material for Baltic birch is sometimes grown on large tree farms. Its quality, however, has dropped in recent years. European plywoods such as Baltic birch are usually produced in 5'-by-5' sheets, whereas most other plywood comes in 4'-by-8' sheets. Other species have been catching up in popularity and are being grown in a sustainable manner on tree farms as well. The species include birch, Italian poplar, and lauan. Any plywood dealer should be able to tell you if the wood came from a certified sustainable source. Also, many manufacturers are now using soy-based non-toxic glues to laminate the layers together.

Commercial plywood, intended for many uses, is made from a variety of wood species and sold in many grades. Construction-grade plywood is usually made from rotary-cut fir, hemlock, and pine. Plywood is categorized from the best grade, A, to grade C, and sometimes D, for the lowest. The grading process considers imperfections, such as knots, voids (surface holes), and checks (open cracks) that are present. Because even at its best, construction-grade plywood is not stable, it is not suitable as a substrate for veneering (**Figure 4-4**). The top layers are so thick they will permit seasonal movement, and the softwoods used are often not strong enough for a good glue bond with the veneer.

Bending Plywood

When layers of wood are glued together in a curved form, the resulting piece is much stronger than the same shape constructed of solid wood. Later in this book we will construct shop-made bent plywood panels, using bending plywood as shown in **Figure 4-5** and **4-6**. Commercially made curved substrates of plywood are also available in many radiuses, sizes, and shapes.

Plywood meant for bending is commonly referred to as bender board and is usually constructed of three layers of lauan. The outer layers are relatively thick and have the same grain direction. The center layer is thinner and has an opposing grain. When bent across grain, the relative open grain of lauan curves easily. The thin center layer flexes, keeping the panel rigid. The surface veneer often needs to be crossbanded; otherwise, the open grain on the convex side can telegraph through to the surface veneer. Bender board is available with the grain direction traveling along the length, referred to as a 4'-by-8' sheet, or with the grain traveling across the width, an 8'-by-4' sheet (sometimes called a barrel). Gluing and stacking sheets of ⅛"-thick plywood in a mold is also a good way to create curved forms.

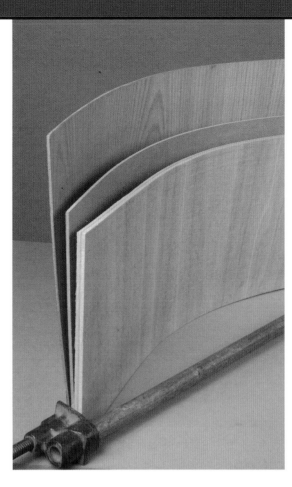

Figure 4-5. Thin plywood panels are easy to bend for creating and veneering curved surfaces. The front panel, called bending ply, has two thick outer layers and a thin center layer.

Figure 4-6. The bent furniture parts were made by gluing veneer onto cores made of bending plywood.

Selecting Plywood

Although plywood is constructed of opposing layers of laminations, the surface veneer still can move just a little and can come loose from the core, or delaminate. It is important to inspect any substrate material for voids and delamination before you use it. Voids repaired at the factory with football shaped patches on the outside skin of plywood are unacceptable, as the shape will telegraph through the veneer to the surface. Look for delamination of the surface veneer and between the core layers of all plywood before using it. Materials with defects are too difficult to repair properly in the shop and should be returned to the supplier for a replacement.

The disadvantages of plywood as a substrate include its surface movement, which can allow surface veneers to crack or separate. The panels can also bow and twist due to slight irregularities. Also, some veneer pattern designs may have grain that runs in several directions, preventing 100% cross-grain lamination.

Composite Substrates

Composite materials such as MDF are excellent substrates for veneering. MDF is a homogeneous material, meaning it has no grain direction at all, although it does vary in density from the surface to the interior. On a homogeneous substrate, the face veneer grain can travel in any combination of directions.

Composite materials resulted from the need to dispose of sawdust, planer shavings, and scraps of wood created by sawmilling and other wood-milling operations. Many of the composite materials are not suitable as substrates for veneering. These include oriented strand board (OSB), made up of layers of large strands of wood fibers or flakes stacked in opposing layers for strength, and wafer board, similar to OSB but without the opposing layers. OSB usually is used for building construction and is too unstable and soft for a veneer substrate. Similarly, wafer board

also is too unstable. Another type of unsuitable composite is hardboard, sometimes called high-density fiberboard or Masonite, which usually has some type of slick finished surface that will not glue well to the veneer.

Particleboard

Particleboard is used as a veneer substrate in large-scale manufacturing operations due to its low cost and relative strength. It is made from varying sizes of wood particles, usually with larger particles near the center of a panel and smaller particles near the surface. For use as a substrate for veneering, it must be cabinet-grade or furniture-grade particleboard, not construction or underlayment grade, which have a coarser surface and are softer.

Medium-Density Fiberboard

I prefer to use the more recently developed MDF, which is made of finer particles than particleboard and has more surface strength and stability (**Figure 4-7**). MDF is a good substrate for many veneering projects, as it can be curved when purchased in ⅛" thickness. Its main disadvantage is its weight. The weight really can add up when constructing a cabinet of several large panels. I often use MDF for tabletops, however, because it seems to make panels feel harder, denser, and more solid.

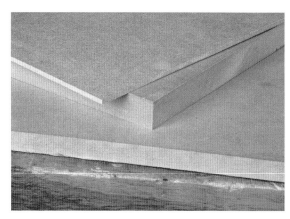

Figure 4-7. MDF is available in many thicknesses, including a ⅛" sheet suitable for bending.

Lumber Core

The third type of manufactured substrate material is lumber core, shown in the chapter opening photo on page 44. Lumber core, in one form or another, has been used for a long time. Some pieces I constructed using lumber core more than 20 years ago have held up extremely well. Lumber core consists of square or rectangular strips of solid wood laid side by side, which are then covered with two or three opposing layers of veneer on each face. There is a small gap left between each strip of the core lumber so it can expand and contract without affecting the surface of the sheet. Lumber core is extremely strong. It is a great choice for shelves and tabletops that must span long distances without support. The strips of wood must be oriented so their length spans the unsupported distance. Doing so creates the strength that would be achieved from a solid board and adds some of the strength of a torsion box. Lumber core itself is heavy and can be expensive, but it is well worth it in the right application.

Torsion Box

A torsion box is simply a core grid of wood strips covered with a skin. The assembly derives tremendous strength from the fact that force applied to the material in any one area is transferred over a much larger area along glue lines in two or more directions (the same principle that makes an airplane wing light yet strong). The torsion box principle is used to create large, sturdy veneered forms that remain relatively light in weight. The surface, or skin, typically consists of ⅛", ¼", or ⅜" plywood or MDF, covered with face veneer.

DEMONSTRATION PROJECT:
The Tabletop Substrate

I have selected MDF as my substrate for the tabletop. It will allow the grain of veneer to run in several directions at once. I want my table solid, so weight is not an issue. There will be a lot of use near the edge, so I will apply a solid wood edge after the panel is glued up (see Chapter 7 for various edging options). I'll also apply a veneer to the back of the substrate, both for looks and for stability.

Honeycomb

The torsion box principle is applied to other light and relatively inexpensive sheet goods suitable for substrates. Honeycomb sheet is one such material. Several types are available, usually constructed of an interior grid of plastic or, increasingly, some type of recycled, soy- or corn-based material. The core is then covered with paper and veneer. The composition reduces the overall weight and is a good option for covering large areas, such as veneer-paneled rooms.

Kerfcore

Another similar, inexpensive material used for bending is Kerfcore. It is made on the same principle as kerf-cutting lumber. Strips of MDF are laid side-by-side with a small gap alongside each and then covered with a thick paper backing on both sides. To prepare the material for use, the paper on one side is slit in between the strips using a special roller. The material can bend easily because one face is still secured, and the other face is free to bend. Kerfcore often is stacked in layers to create a sandwich. A similar product that recently appeared on the market is kerf-cut MDF. Most of the man-made materials do not have a solid surface, so crossbanding helps to create the illusion of solid wood, particularly when the materials are touched or knocked with a knuckle.

CHAPTER 5

Adhesives

Materials used to glue two pieces of wood together changed little from the times of ancient Egypt until the early twentieth century. All were derived from animals or plants. The glues were made of bones, hide, albumin, casein, and various vegetable mixtures. Because these were organic in nature, they would succumb over time to a combination of moisture, heat, and dryness. Both the expense of making the glues and their long-term ineffectiveness meant that they were not always an option, and therefore, many types of wood joinery were developed that did not require any glue. Clever joinery, however, was not an option for veneering applications—veneers were usually attached using hide glue. Many antiques in my shop had only dust where the hide glue was originally, until I reglued the veneer.

Long-lasting synthetic glues began to be developed during the first part of the 20th century. The new glues were increasingly resistant to water and heat, making them excellent for veneering.

Veneer craftsmen buy
glue in gallon bottles.

Synthetic glues

Man-made glues can be grouped into two broad categories: thermosetting and thermoplastic. Thermosetting glues cure by heat, by some kind of chemical reaction, or by a mixture of both. Thermosetting glues create a stronger bond than thermoplastic glues because a more complex 3-D network of bonded molecules results from the chemical reaction. Once cured, the process is not reversible. Thermosetting adhesives include resorcinol, epoxy, and urea formaldehyde. Thermosetting glues usually need to be mixed with water or another chemical to initiate the chemical reaction that causes them to set. To prevent the glue from setting up before application, many are sold in two parts. The chemicals involved are toxic to some extent.

Thermoplastics are condensation polymers that cure when a molecule, usually water, is released. Because they cure by evaporation, most of them will soften to some extent if you apply water and heat. Thermoplastic adhesives include most common types of white and yellow glues for woodworking and carpentry. They generally are easy to use because they can be applied right from the container and allowed to dry. Thermoplastic glues also can be cured using heat because the heat quickens the release of the water molecules. Some thermoplastics, including Titebond II and Titebond III, create an interlocking molecular network very similar in strength to that of thermosetting glues, but can be remelted. Thermoplastics are generally non-toxic.

Within the two broad groupings are many different adhesives that will securely bond veneer with a substrate. No single glue is suited to every application, so a good knowledge of a variety of glues is essential.

Choosing glue

Numerous factors should be considered when choosing glue for a specific application including open time and the environment of the piece, the glue's ability to bond with and/or seep through the substrate and veneer, and its environmental impact.

The open time of a glue dictates how much time you have from when you apply the glue until the veneer is in place and pressure is applied. Open time varies, depending on the temperature and humidity in the workshop.

The environment of the piece, where and how it will be used, and whether it will be exposed to heat, sunlight, or unusually heavy use, determines whether the glue needs to be water resistant or waterproof.

The glue's effect on different materials indicates whether or not it will be able to make a strong bond with both the substrate and the veneer. A characteristic affected by the openness of the pores in the wood veneer you are using is whether the glue will seep through the veneer and stain the surface or interfere with finishing.

Toxicity is an additional concern both as it relates to the maker and to the end user.

Some people are very sensitive to chemicals in resorcinol, epoxy, and urea formaldehyde glue. Some glues can leave chemical residues that linger for a long time. There may also be environmental concerns about the way the glue was manufactured or how it will affect the environment once the piece is completed.

The following list provides some background information on a variety of glues.

Hide glue

Hide glue, made by rendering hides, hooves, and other various combinations of animal parts, is the oldest glue still in use for veneering. Usually sold in the form of crystals or beads, it is mixed with water and heated either in a double boiler or in a glue pot. It also is available pre-mixed in squeeze bottles. Hide glue is good for veneering. It can be applied using an iron and a veneer hammer, instead of using clamps. There's a detailed description of the process in Chapter 6. The same method can be used for applying veneers with PVA glues as well, with good results.

The problem with hide glue for veneering is its reversibility—it will soften and release if it becomes wet and also may deteriorate with age. The very factors that make hide glue troublesome for veneering, however, make it ideal for other applications, such as building stringed musical instruments. Musical instruments will not be exposed to excessive moisture, heat, or sunlight, and it is advantageous to be able to 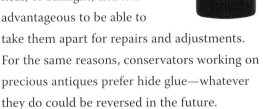 take them apart for repairs and adjustments. For the same reasons, conservators working on precious antiques prefer hide glue—whatever they do could be reversed in the future.

PVA glue

The most commonly used type of adhesive in small woodworking operations is polyvinyl acetate (PVA) glue. The category includes white glue (aliphatic resin), yellow glue (also aliphatic resin), and cross-linking PVA glues such as Titebond II. One thing all PVA glues have in common is a relatively short open time, five to twelve minutes, often less if the weather is very warm. Also, they do not set properly in a cold workshop when the wood is colder than about 50° F. When assembling larger, more complicated projects, additional open time is important. Some veneers, such as rosewood and teak, have an oily surface that does not bond well with PVA glues.

White PVA Glue

White glue, such as Elmer's, is commonly used in schools and for craft projects: It is inexpensive, it bonds well, and it is easy to clean up with soap and water. For wood projects, it bonds in a relatively short amount of time; however, it remains slightly pliable after it dries and can permit what woodworkers call joint creep. A little joint creep can be an advantage when one bonded material may need to move slightly in relation to the other due to seasonal changes. Unfortunately, joint creep may allow the surface of the veneer to crack, split, or separate, so in most cases, there needs to be a firmer bond to prevent movement. White glue has an open time of around five minutes, shorter if the workshop is very warm.

Yellow PVA Glue

The second type of PVA is more suited to most woodworking and many veneering projects. Originated by the Franklin Company, Titebond, or yellow glue, is an aliphatic resin glue with a similar chemical make-up to white glue. Titebond has improved water resistance and dries harder, resulting in less joint creep and better sandability. The yellow color is the result of dyes the manufacturer adds to set it apart from white glue and helps to hide glue lines in lighter woods. The glue also is available in darker colors for use with darker woods and, like most glues covered in this book, can be tinted with aniline dyes or with other types of stains and pigments. That becomes important with some veneers because glue can be forced up to the surface during gluing. Yellow glue usually has an open time of five to ten minutes and will not set properly in a cold workshop.

Cross-Linking PVA Glue

The Franklin Company also introduced cross-linking polyvinyl acetate. This more advanced type of PVA contains a self-linking polymer that does not require additional chemicals to set. The polymer makes the glue stronger and more water resistant; as a result, it has replaced regular yellow glue in many woodworking shops.

Cross-linking PVA glue is customized to have diverse characteristics, such as a

longer open time, increased water resistance, better gap-filling ability, and darker color, and each formula is sold under a different brand name. The glues have a good balance of strength, ease of application and cleanup, cost, and versatility. The open time for these modified PVA glues ranges from five to twelve minutes, depending on the temperature of the shop. Like the other PVA glues, they do not set well in cold workshops.

A modified PVA specifically formulated for wood veneer, Titebond Cold Press for Veneer, was introduced by the Franklin Company. It has similar qualities to the glue described above but with minimal bleed-through, even with open-grained woods, and is light brown in color. More recently, the company came out with an advanced formula sold as Titebond III, which combines many of the desirable characteristics of Franklin's previous glues into one formula. Titebond III has a relatively long open time, is water resistant, and dries hard with a minimum of joint creep. It dries hard enough to use for bent panels without the curve relaxing, provided the curve does not have an extremely small radius. Its main drawback is that it dries to a dark brown color.

Urea formaldehyde glue

Urea formaldehyde glues allow for more open time. This comes in handy when constructing bend laminations with several layers that need to be glued at the same time, placing multiple panels in the press at the same time, and making other complex projects. The open time provided by urea formaldehyde is also useful when you want to adjust the veneers after they are laid down. It must remain clamped under pressure for 24 hours to set up properly at room temperature. In an industrial setting that uses hot pressing technology, heat can speed up the setting

process to as little as a few minutes. Many types of plywood and composite board are manufactured with urea formaldehyde glue, so it is a safe bet it will adhere to them. The glue is produced in one- and two-part mixes.

Urea formaldehyde is a known carcinogen, and the powder will set when exposed to any moisture, including the moisture in your lungs.

Always wear a dust mask when using either type of urea formaldehyde glue. The glue also will set under water, so waste glue should never be put down the drain. Other than that, the glue is easy to clean up with soap and water before it sets, is relatively easy to use, and bonds veneer well to a variety of surfaces. It can be spread with a roller brush or notched trowel. Urea formaldehyde glue usually dries to a tan in color, fine for most woods.

One-Part Urea Formaldehyde

One-part urea formaldehyde glue consists of a single powder to mix with water. The most widely used brand is Weldwood Plastic Resin glue. It bonds well with most wood-based materials and oily veneers, allows little or no joint creep, is heat and somewhat water resistant, and has average gap-filling abilities. The glue can be sensitive to heat in liquid form, an advantage in some situations. In a cool shop, for example, its open time can be increased to as much as 45 minutes. It needs to stay

clamped for 12 to 24 hours to fully set in normal conditions, but increased shop temperatures will help it to set up much quicker. One-part urea formaldehyde glue is also available in a formula specifically made for veneer, Pro Glue Veneer Bond Adhesive, manufactured by Vac-U-Clamp.

Two-Part Urea Formaldehyde

The stronger and more durable type of urea formaldehyde glue is packaged in two parts: a powder resin and a powder or liquid hardener to mix for use. Two-part urea formaldehyde glue often is used in hot pressing applications. It also has many characteristics that make it useful in the small workshop. As with one-part urea formaldehyde resin, two-part has a long open time, which can be increased through slight cooling. Also, like the one-part formula, two-part has excellent creep and heat resistance, although it has better moisture resistance. Two-part gains increased gap-filling capabilities by mixing about 5% by weight of a little wheat and nut flour to the hardener before mixing it with the resin. The addition helps when gluing down open-grained veneers or veneers with slight defects: When the glue bleeds through to the surface, it will fill very small holes.

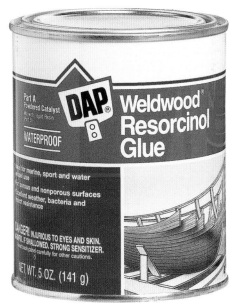

Resorcinol glue

Resorcinol glue is very resistant to moisture and is commonly used in exterior construction and boat building. Resorcinol is packaged in two parts, a liquid resin in a water-alcohol solution and a dry hardener. Open time is usually about 10 minutes, which can be increased by cooling the wood below 70° F. The glue also cleans up with soap and water before it sets and can be applied by brush, roller, notched trowel, or spray gun. Resorcinol leaves a slightly darker glue line than urea formaldehyde, so take care when using it with light-colored woods.

Epoxy

Epoxy has tremendous holding strength, resists moisture well, has excellent gap-filling ability, and can bond with almost any surface. Once set it does not dissolve or soften. It does tend to bleed up to the surface of many veneers, which causes extra cleanup. It fills gaps well and, if colored, can be useful for veneers with slight surface defects. Just as with urea formaldehyde glue, epoxy can fill the surface of open-grained veneer from below.

A good rule of thumb when selecting epoxy is the faster the setting time, the lower the quality of the bond. Fast-setting epoxies have a lower ratio of bonding resin to hardener than do epoxies with long curing times. As a result, the slow-setting epoxies are much harder when fully set. For veneering applications, epoxies are available that have up to 70 minutes of working time. Even longer open time can be achieved by increasing the workshop temperature to 75° F or higher.

Alone, epoxy has excellent gap-filling abilities, and it can also be mixed with sawdust from the wood that you are bonding, or with colored wood flour, without a significant decrease in strength. Very fine dust mixed with epoxy will create a nice uniform color when the filled area is sanded and finished. I save a little sawdust of each species of wood from the bag of my finish sander to have for mixing with epoxy. Dust from a saw or rough sander is too coarse. It will show up as little dots in a field of clear epoxy.

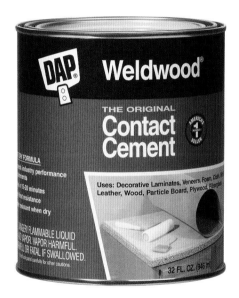

Contact cement

Contact cement can be used for limited veneering applications. Contact cement is difficult to use when laying down sheets of unbacked veneer because it will not allow the veneer to move at all, making it virtually impossible to roll out any wrinkles or bubbles without destroying the veneer. After it has cured, however, contact cement remains just slightly rubbery, allowing for joint creep. Contact cement can be used to apply veneer to a wide surface that cannot be clamped, put into a vacuum bag, or hammer veneered. That is the case with a complex curve, part of an existing piece of furniture that defies clamping, or when on-site away from the shop. The fumes from most contact cements are toxic and flammable. They must be used with a proper respirator and adequate ventilation.

The best way to use contact cement is to create a rigid sheet of laid-up veneer that has been crossbanded using another type of glue. The resulting sheet will be thick and rigid enough to lie down flat when it is applied with contact cement, in the same manner as plastic laminate sheets. Contact cement is excellent for applying man-made veneers, such as Treefrog and others that have a phenolic backer (the same backer used for plastic laminates).

It's very tricky to keep a demo project like our tabletop marching in perfect sequence with the surrounding text, and the truth is, I had to make two tabletops. You'll no doubt notice a burl inlay has suddenly appeared in the shot and taped-up field veneer that I'm gluing down, even though I don't discuss inlay techniques until Chapter 9.

I'm using Titebond III for the tabletop project because it is harder and more water resistant than the other formulations. Spread the glue on the substrate (Figure 5-3) but not on the veneers. If you spread glue on the veneers, they will curl up and become impossible to press down.

Step 1. Carefully place the taped layup on the glue. Align the layup with the edges of the substrate. The last opportunity to manipulate it is at hand.

Step 2. Immediately spritz distilled water over the entire top surface. That will prevent the veneer from curling up (from the glue moisture on its other side) before you get it into the press.

FSV Adhesives

For applying paper-backed sheet veneers, there are flexible sheet veneer (FSV) adhesives, which are applied in the same way as contact cement. They allow the veneer to be repositioned or removed for up to 10 minutes before they begin to set. FSV adhesive is applied with a foam roller to the substrate only, which prevents the veneer from curling. Once the sheet veneer has been positioned, it is rolled out using a rubber roller, similar to the process when using contact cement. Once cured, FSV adhesives allow much less joint creep than contact cement.

Glue sheets

Another way to attach veneer is to use glue sheets. A sheet of glue is placed between the substrate and the veneer. The veneer is ironed down with the heat from an iron, melting the glue and then setting it. Veneers that already have adhesives on them also are available at most woodworking supply stores. Pre-applied adhesives are either iron-on or have a self-sticking adhesive with a backer that peels off. The self-adhesive veneers are available only in a few selected species, and the options for matching them often are limited.

Spreading glue

There can be a lot of surface to cover with glue, and a finger or little flat stick will not work. You can use a paint roller, but I prefer a notched trowel with $\frac{1}{16}$" notches. I often file the tops of the notches down to around one-half their original height, creating lines of glue that are $\frac{1}{16}$" wide by $\frac{1}{32}$" high (**Figure 5-1**). That size seems to be the perfect amount of glue for veneering (**Figure 5-2**). The glue must be carefully combed lengthwise and crosswise (**Figure 5-3**): Too much glue will cause ripples under the surface, while not enough glue will cause bubbles in the spots where the veneer did not adhere. A disposable trim roller is handy for spreading glue on strips of veneer for edging (**Figure 5-4**).

The glue should be applied only to the substrate, not the veneer, except in hammer veneering, when glue must be spread on both surfaces. Placing one side of the veneer into the glue will cause it to curl up even before it can be pressed down. Spray a little water on the top surface of the veneer, just after placing it on the glue. That way both sides of the veneer will have a little moisture on them, reducing any curl until things are lined up and ready to clamp.

Oily Veneers

When using particularly oily veneers, such as vintage Brazilian rosewood, wipe them with a rag slightly moistened in acetone to remove most of the oily residue from the surface to be glued. The acetone will evaporate quickly and will not interfere with adhesion the way paint thinner or lacquer thinner could.

Normally, I use Titebond II or Titebond III for gluing down veneer, but for the small percentage of oily veneers (mostly rosewood and teak), urea-based glues, such as Weldwood plastic resin glue or Pro-Glue veneer bond dry resin, will work better. With some of the glues, the oil will not have to be removed from the surface. Urea-based glues are not suitable for hammer veneering.

Figure 5-1. Pour a bead of glue on the substrate. Prepare the trowel by filing its finest teeth down to about $\frac{1}{32}$" high.

Figure 5-2. Use a notched trowel to spread and comb the glue into a uniformly thin, wet layer.

Figure 5-3. Spread the glue in one direction, then comb it in the crossways direction. Cover the substrate right out to the edges. Spatula any excess glue back into the bottle.

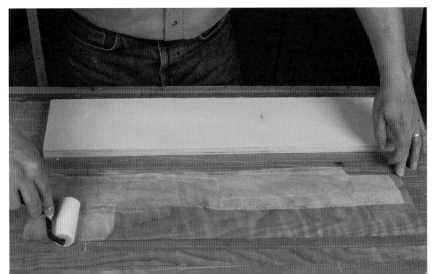

Figure 5-4. A disposable trim roller can spread glue on surfaces too narrow for the notched trowel in preparation for hammer veneering.

CHAPTER 6

Pressure & Presses

"Pressure serves several useful purposes: It forces entrapped air from the joint; it brings adhesive into molecular contact with wood surfaces; it forces adhesive to penetrate into the wood structure for more effective mechanical interlocking." (U.S. Forest Service, Forest Products Laboratory)

After veneer is ready for gluing, there are many ways to press it down. The ancient Egyptians used stones. More recently, large industries have used hydraulic presses that set the glue very quickly with heat or radio waves. But, since before the Industrial Revolution, smaller woodworking operations used presses featuring screws made of wood or metal. In the mid-1980s, vacuum presses began to replace screw presses in many small workshops.

For anyone starting out with veneering, a few clamps and cauls (thick pieces of wood to help distribute clamping pressure) will do the job nicely. Another method, hammer veneering, does away with the press entirely, relying instead on the localized pressure exerted by a narrow iron tool. Hammer veneering is covered in detail on page 72.

All pressing processes can be used to create curved forms as well as flat panels. What they all have in common is uniform pressure must be applied to the entire veneer-covered area long enough for the adhesive to set. Uniform pressure will achieve a proper bond between veneer and substrate.

Wooden cauls squeezed by ordinary clamps offer the simplest way to press a veneered panel.

Hot-pressing

Knowing about the process of hot-pressing can help explain the principles behind some veneering operations and show why industry is better at some things and small shops at others. Hot presses are large, expensive, and take up a large amount of space, and for these reasons, are suitable for a large volume of work. Hot presses cannot stop, change gears, and start over again, but they are ideal for covering many sheets of material with similar veneer quickly and at a relatively low cost. Large hydraulic presses also can produce a great amount of curved work. The curved shapes are manufactured in various contours and radiuses and are available with raw or already veneered surfaces.

A small shop can use a limited amount of carefully matched veneer for small projects, doing the work more efficiently using clamps and press screws. The two methods are often combined. For example, cherry cabinets built using pre-veneered plywood from a manufacturer can be faced with attractively matched veneers done in the shop.

Factory-made pre-veneered flat panels have veneer applied to either plywood or MDF. For lower grades of surfaces, rotary-cut veneer is clipped to size, ready to apply. For higher grades of surfaces, veneer is sorted by hand or machine and joined using fiberglass string by a machine called a veneer stitcher. The fiberglass string replaces the paper veneer tape a handworker would use. Glue is then spread on the substrate in a curtain of adhesive by spray, roller, foaming, or an extrusion of narrow, evenly spaced lines of glue that flow out to a consistent thickness under pressure—kind of like an automated notched trowel.

Once glued, the veneer is placed on the substrate, and the panel is cold-pressed to spread the glue, flatten the veneer, and remove any excess air trapped under the surface. Too much pressure forces too much glue into the wood fiber, causing the joint to be starved of glue. Too little pressure allows the air bubbles to become trapped under the surface. Too much pressure is not an issue in small-shop operations because small-shop equipment cannot produce the amount of pressure that hydraulic presses can. Note, however, that softer woods may require less pressure to force the proper amount of adhesive down into the grain of the wood, and harder, denser woods may take more pressure for a proper bond.

After cold-pressing, heat is applied at temperatures ranging up to 165° C or 325° F, for anywhere from two to fifteen minutes. A radio-frequency heated press can accelerate the setting time by focusing energy right on the glue line. The panel is then set aside to cure for a time depending on the adhesive used, the moisture content of the wood, and atmospheric conditions.

Pressing T E R M S

Bending form. A wooden mold, made in one part for vacuum bag pressing and two parts for use with clamps and screws, is a bending form and presses veneers and suitable substrates together to take on the curve of the mold.

Caul. A flat piece of wood or one with a bowed center, helps distribute clamping pressure across a veneered panel. The caul also keeps the press screws from direct contact with the delicate veneer.

Clamping beam. A heavy wooden caul used to distribute pressure across a veneer glue-up is a clamping beam.

Hot press. An industrial veneer press used to set glue very quickly is called a hot press. It has heated platens, a radio-frequency heating apparatus, or both.

Pressure fan, pressure cone. Pressure from a clamp or veneer screw fans out in a 45-degree cone from the point of application—this is called a pressure fan. Inserting a thick caul between the screw and the workpiece helps distribute the pressure.

Springback. The tendency of bent wood, including glued-up bent laminations, to give up some of their curvature upon being released from a bending form is known as spring back.

Veneer hammer. A hand tool used to squeegee veneer down tight is a veneer hammer. The tool usually is used in conjunction with a hot iron that melts the glue.

Pressing Concerns

To achieve a smooth, void-free surface when clamping or pressing down veneer, there are two main considerations: smooth clamps and cauls, and uniform clamping pressure.

Any surface that comes into contact with the veneer as it is setting needs to be clean, smooth, and as uniform as possible. For all clamping and pressing techniques, there must be some sort of pad right over the veneer. Any irregularities on the pad's surface will transmit onto the surface of the veneer. Any pieces of dirt, dried glue, or foreign matter trapped under the pad will emboss its shape into the surface of the veneer.

Melamine and MDF both work very well as clamp pads. They have a smooth and uniform surface that stays firm, even under great pressure. Always place clean newsprint, not printed newspaper, between the surface of the veneer and the pad to prevent them from bonding together. Preventing bonding allows the pads to be reused many times.

The second consideration is applying uniform pressure over the entire surface. Clamps will work if you can spread the pressure out beyond the points of pressure created by the clamps themselves. This can be accomplished by the use of cauls and boards (**Figure 6-1**). The pressure radiates out at a 45-degree angle from the pad of each clamp, forming a cone shape. To prevent areas from not receiving enough pressure, causing voids or bubbles, make sure each cone of pressure overlaps the one next to it.

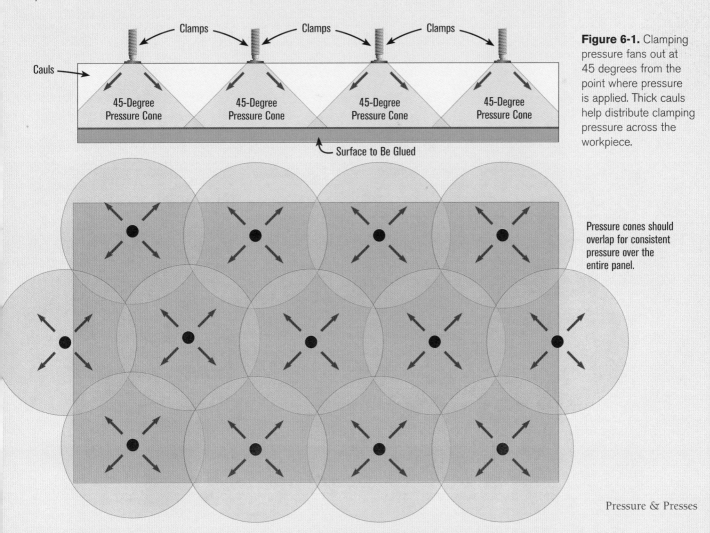

Figure 6-1. Clamping pressure fans out at 45 degrees from the point where pressure is applied. Thick cauls help distribute clamping pressure across the workpiece.

Pressure cones should overlap for consistent pressure over the entire panel.

Clamps and cauls

Most shops contain a number of clamps, so I will begin by discussing how to press down veneer using clamps with cauls, as shown in the photo on page 62. When teaching, I introduce veneering by making 12"-by-12" panels pressed using clamps. The process is a great way to get a feel for veneering and to learn the basic techniques of cutting, matching, gluing, and pressing without investing a large amount of time and money. The panels can be used for box tops, doors, or veneered samples to show potential clients. You can go on to create some large panels using clamps and cauls.

Veneered panels typically are much wider than the throat depth of any clamps. The solution is to bridge the panel with thick cauls or clamping beams, which are slightly bowed. When each caul is clamped at both ends, the clamping pressure forces the bow out of the caul. This applies pressure to the center of the panel and extends it out toward the edges. Use the principle of overlap described in the sidebar on page 65 to evenly distribute the pressure over the entire surface.

Apply the same principles of uniform pressure and smooth cauls to the bottom of the panel to be veneered as well, even if you are only veneering one side. Otherwise, you may defeat the purpose of applying uniform pressure to the top. You should be able to stack two panels together with a pad between them if you wish. As you add more layers needing to be pressed together, however, more and more pressure must be added. This becomes difficult with common clamps.

Curved work can also be pressed with clamps if you make a suitably curved form with curved cauls tailored to the work, **Figure 6-2**.

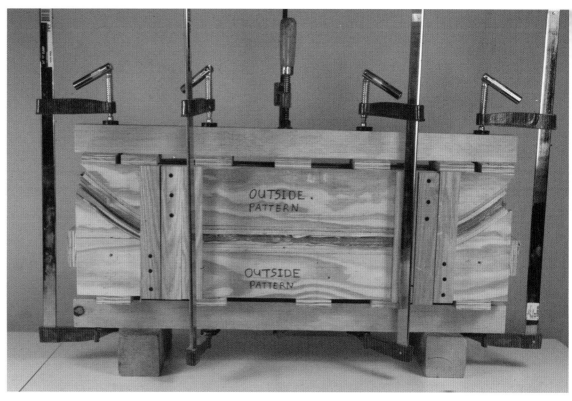

Figure 6-2. With a suitable bending form, cabinetmaking clamps are capable of bending a curved veneer layup as easily as a straight one. The vertical keys on the sides of the form help align its top and bottom halves.

Figure 6-3. Place the veneered panel on an MDF platen and slide it into the screw press. Space the screws across each press section to deliver uniform pressure over the entire panel.

Screw press

The screw press takes the clamps-and-cauls process a step further. The apparatus consists of several coarse-threaded clamping screws mounted in a stout wood or steel frame (**Figure 6-3**) and tightened down over the work. Additional frames allow the pressure to be applied to a panel of almost any size. Loading the press requires spacing the bottom beams to accommodate the panel. The beams are covered first with an MDF platen, then the workpiece, then a protective sheet of clean newsprint, then a top platen (**Figure 6-4**), and, finally, the top beams (**Figure 6-5**), which transmit the pressure from the screws to the panel. The top beams also shorten the distance the screws must be turned, eliminating a lot of tiring twisting (**Figure 6-6**).

Some details of the press, which I built myself, are shown in **Figure 6-7**. The press framework has to be strong enough to remain rigid when the pressure is applied. Press screws of various lengths are readily available and can be used along with angle iron and channel iron to construct a shop-made press. I use the screw press method in my shop almost exclusively. The press is always set up and ready, is easy to load, has few parts to fail, allows air to circulate around the work during the drying process, and can provide a great deal of pressure when and where needed. Curved work can also be veneered in a screw press with a suitably curved form and curved cauls tailored to the work (**Figure 6-8**).

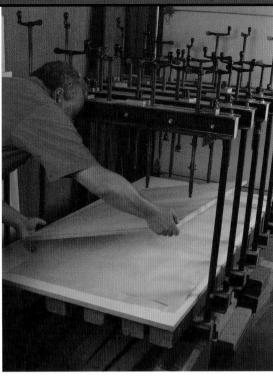

Figure 6-4. Cover the veneer with clean newsprint, then a platen of MDF. The shop-made press can accommodate work up to 6' long and 36" wide.

Figure 6-5. Space the top beams across the panel, then begin tightening the press screws in the center section. Tighten across the section and then retighten each screw.

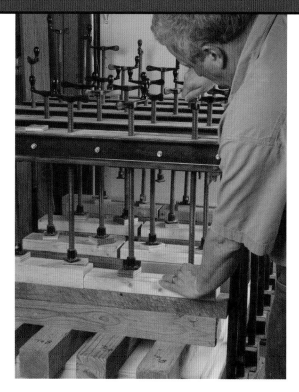

Figure 6-6. Work systematically from the center of the press toward both ends, adding blocks as needed.

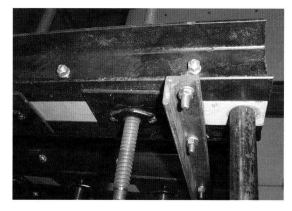

Figure 6-7. The nuts for the press screws are screwed to the bottom of the maple beams. Bolts sandwich each beam between two large pieces of channel iron, with angle iron tying the sections together.

Figure 6-8. A large screw press like this, which the author built for himself, can accommodate jigs for laminate bending as easily as flat work.

Vacuum bag press

The vacuum bag press is probably the most widely used in tool small shops today for pressing down veneer. Its ease of use, low cost, versatility, and ability to be easily stored have made it popular very quickly (**Figure 6-9**).

The principle of vacuum bag veneering harnesses the weight of the atmosphere on the outside of a thick plastic bag, and thus on the workpiece inside the bag, by removing all air from inside the bag. The pressure inside the bag is similar to the pressure when diving deep under water and is tremendous: 14.7 pounds per square inch, or 2,117 pounds per square foot, at sea level. This pressure drops off at elevations of more than 5,000 feet, however. Because the pressure is applied to all sides uniformly, the vacuum bag press is ideal for curved work. There are several types of systems available, but they all work in essentially the same way.

To use a vacuum bag system, you must first make a flat platen of Melamine with a grid work of grooves cut on the table saw (**Figure 6-10**). Drill a hole in the edge that connects to one of the grooves on the surface. The air will flow through the grid work of grooves, through the drilled hole, and then out of the bag through a tube connected to the vacuum pump (**Figure 6-11**).

Figure 6-9. The vacuum pump, right, draws the air out of the heavy plastic bag that encloses the veneered panel. Channels sawn in the lower platen draw the air from everywhere in the bag; the pressure gauge monitors the process. With the bag evacuated, the atmosphere exerts pressure of almost 15 pounds per square inch across the entire panel.

Figure 6-10. The Melamine platen has a grid of air-evacuation channels sawn across its entire surface.

Figure 6-11. The vacuum pump's hose feeds through a valve in the plastic bag into a hole connecting to the air evacuation channels. A small hose clamp tightens the hose in place.

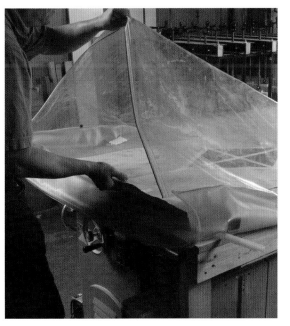

Figure 6-12. After spreading glue on the substrate and spritzing the top veneers with distilled water, slide the panel into the vacuum bag.

Figure 6-13. This bag closes by pressing a tube over the bag end into a mating channel. A tight seal is essential.

Figure 6-14. As the pump draws the vacuum, the bag flattens over the panel. Encourage it with a hard rubber roller, which also can be used to flatten any glue puddles that form.

Figure 6-15. The vacuum bag can pull veneers over a one-piece curved form, though you will need to encourage the bend as the vacuum is drawn.

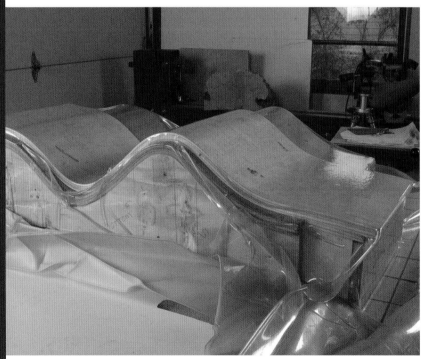

Figure 6-16. The bag press successfully pulls the veneer layers down onto the bending form.

The bag is either sealed up on the ends or on the top for easier loading (**Figure 6-12**). Bags are available in various shapes and sizes or can be created by using vinyl adhesive and a seam roller to seal the edges. A simple tube-and-U-channel system closes the loading end of the bag (**Figure 6-13**). The operator needs to monitor the process as the pump draws the vacuum, removing folds from the bag and encouraging it to tighten uniformly over the workpiece. A hard rubber roller can be used to smooth out any bubbles in the bag or any glue puddles that form under the veneer—you'll be able to feel them with your fingertips (**Figure 6-14**).

For most curved work, you will need a one-part form (**Figure 6-15**) with a thin flexible caul over the top of the veneer to prevent bubbles and wrinkles (**Figure 6-16**). The form has to be sturdy with a network of holes drilled to allow the air to easily pass through it, otherwise the form will collapse under pressure. The grid work platen described above for flat work can be replaced with a flexible mesh that allows the entire bag to bend around a form or a series of sticks. The addition of flexible mesh is an excellent method for creating curved stair stringers and other curvilinear shapes.

The smooth, flat caul over the top of the veneer should be the same size as the panel to be veneered. If the caul is too big, the overhanging area will break off under the pressure of the bag. If it is too small, it will leave unpressed veneer around the edges of the panel. Also, be sure to round over any sharp edges of the caul and platen to prevent the edges and corners from ripping the bag.

Hammer veneering

Clamps, the screw press, and the vacuum press each apply pressure to the entire panel, all at once. The traditional veneer hammer can achieve a secure bond by applying highly localized pressure (**Figure 6-17**). In the traditional version of the technique, the hammer is used with hot hide glue. In the contemporary version, as shown in the step-by-step sequence on page 72, regular yellow woodworking glue is used. (I prefer Titebond II.)

A veneer hammer isn't really a hammer—it's more like a squeegee. It allows the application of very concentrated pressure along a narrow line, which encourages the glued veneer to bond to the substrate below. The veneer hammer resembles an adze: a steel head set crossways to its handle. The head is between 3" and 4" wide with a thick, rounded blade and a heavy poll that can be grasped to apply pressure. Veneer hammers also can be made out of any fine-grained hardwood, though beech is traditional. Cut a slot in the head for the blade itself, which can be a strip of steel or brass.

The key is to spread glue on both the veneer and the substrate and then allow the glue to dry enough to skin over before you bond it with the hot iron and the veneer hammer. The time can vary significantly, depending on the local temperature and humidity. When the glue is ready and at its most flexible, it turns from a creamy white to a dark yellow color. A finger should slide right over the glue without sticking. At that point, the glue is dry enough to remelt easily without a lot of messy liquid.

The panel shown in the step-by-step sequence is a small plywood shelf, but there is no limit to the size of the workpiece that can be hammer veneered. The technique also works very well on curved surfaces, as you will see in Chapter 12. In **Figure 6-18**, the completed panel has been moistened with water both to show how it will look when finished and to help find and repair any air bubbles under the veneer (Chapter 8).

Figure 6-17. The veneer hammer, over the area of its small, narrow face, can apply tremendous pressure to the veneer. Working the hammer over the veneer surface spreads the pressure to the entire panel. This shop-made version of the veneer hammer, top, was assembled from plumbing parts and a 3" brick chisel.

Figure 6-18. A hammer-veneered panel has been moistened with distilled water, to show how it will look when finished.

Hammer veneering is an old technique that does away with the need for clamps and presses. Instead, a narrow-faced hammer is used like a squeegee to apply concentrated pressure, along with a hot iron to melt the glue in the work zone.

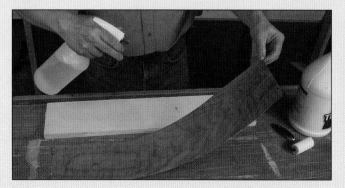

Step 1. Spritz the show side of the veneer with distilled water; then, roll a uniform spread of glue on both the veneer and the substrate.

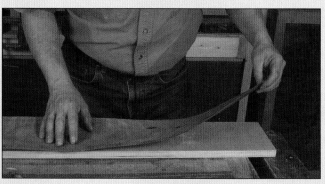

Step 2. Allow the glue to dry until it visibly skins over, about an hour with most yellow glues. Then, lay the veneer on the substrate and smooth it into place.

Step 3. Press the veneer down with hand pressure. Work over the surface with a hot iron, which remelts the setting glue and begins the bonding process.

Step 4. Press hard on the veneer hammer as you work from the center to the edges of the veneer and push any glue bubbles off the edge. Cover the entire surface.

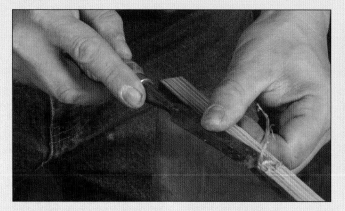

Step 5. Trim the excess veneer with a sharp chisel and sand the edge flat, being careful not to round the corners.

Step 6. Use the iron and the veneer hammer to press the edge veneer onto the substrate. Trim with a chisel and sand smooth.

Trimming veneered panels

Once the adhesive has set and the panel has been removed from the press, there are several methods for trimming the panel to size without damaging the surface veneer. The surface veneers can be quite delicate at this stage, so it's important to proceed carefully. The first step is to measure exactly where you intend to cut. In panels with a centered motif or a centered veneer match, like the one shown in **Figure 6-19**, measure from the central join between the veneers.

These cutting methods make it difficult to protect the fibers of the veneer on the bottom of the panel. A sacrificial board placed under the panel, cut through at the same time as the panel is cut, will go a long way toward solving the problem. A strip of blue painter's tape along the underside of the cut line (**Figure 6-20**) also helps.

Router and Fence

A router with a straight bit can be guided by running the router base along the fence. I prefer to use a four-flute spiral-cutting bit, sometimes referred to as a mill bit. The bit usually will shear the wood fibers off cleanly (**Figure 6-21**). In veneer work, bits with a downward spiral work best. Such bits tend to push the wood fibers down onto the substrate instead of pulling them up. Bits with an upward spiral are preferred for mortising, where you want to lift the chips out of the excavation.

Routing can leave the delicate grain along the edge of the veneer vulnerable to tear-out, particularly when cutting end grain or highly figured veneers. If the substrate is plywood, the veneer of the plywood right under the surface veneer may tear out as well. Tape the underside of the cut, and carefully guide the router along a securely clamped metal straightedge (**Figure 6-22**). After routing, finish the edge by sanding with a flat sanding stick (**Figure 6-23**). That will leave a clean edge suitable for applying a veneer or solid-wood edge (Chapter 7).

Figure 6-19. Carefully lay out the trimming cuts, measuring from the center of the veneers.

Figure 6-20. Run a strip of blue painter's tape on the underside of the cut line to help prevent chipping out.

Figure 6-21. For the cleanest cut, mount a downward cutting spiral-fluted router bit.

Figure 6-22. Clamp a metal fence to the panel, and slowly steer the router along it.

Knife, Straightedge, and Router

Another method of cutting a veneered panel to size is to start by placing a wooden straightedge on the surface of the veneer right on the cut line. The fibers of the veneer face can be cut with a sharp knife, to prevent them from tearing out. The straight edge should be made of a good, solid wood and must make contact with the surface of the veneer along the entire length of the cut (**Figure 6-24**). After the knife cut, you can use a bearing-guided following bit in the router to trim off the substrate and the veneer to its finished dimension. A bit with the bearing on either the top or the bottom of the cutter can be used, provided the straightedge remains on the finished A side of the panel to clamp the delicate fibers in place.

Figure 6-23. After routing, finish the edge by sanding with a flat sanding stick.

Figure 6-24. Clamp a metal straightedge on the cut line and score the line with a sharp knife. This will help prevent chipping the face veneers.

Table Saw

A table saw should have a fine, sharp blade raised as high as possible (**Figure 6-25**) to cut a veneered panel to size. A blade set properly and in good condition will cut the wood fibers in a downward direction, pushing them down into the panel. If the blade were low, the teeth of the saw would hit the wood fibers from the side, tearing them away from the cut. Securing the wood fibers down by placing blue painter's tape over the area to be cut also helps.

To protect veneers on the underside of the panel, a table saw with a scoring blade is the best solution. A scoring blade is a small blade that runs in the opposite direction from the main cutting blade. It cleanly shears off the fibers on the underside of the panel before the main blade cuts through the panel. Without a scoring blade, the veneer cut still can be very clean on both sides of the panel by using a spiral-cutting router bit and a fence, as described on page 73, to partially cut through the panel from the B side. Then, turn the panel over and finish sawing it to size.

A sacrificial board under the veneered panel also protects the veneer from tearing out on the underside as it is being cut on the table saw, which works best with a crosscut sled. As with the top surface, it helps to place blue painter's tape along the cut line on the underside, to further protect the delicate fibers of the veneer.

Figure 6-25. The table saw can make a clean trimming cut on a veneered panel. Raise the blade high, use a sliding crosscut box, and tape the cut line on the underside.

DEMONSTRATION PROJECT: Pressing and Trimming the Tabletop

Throughout Chapter 6, you have seen the tabletop demonstration project proceed through the stages of pressing and trimming. One version of the demo tabletop has been pressed in the veneer press, and the other has been in the vacuum bag. It is always a thrill when a newly pressed panel emerges from the press—a beautiful but fragile stack of veneers has been joined into a smooth sheet and adhered to a stout substrate. The transformation is magical (**Figure 6-26**).

Figure 6-26. A newly pressed panel emerges from the veneer press.

CHAPTER 7

The Edge

Before applying the veneer to a substrate, you need to consider what type of edge your panel will have. The decision is important to make before you apply the veneer because in many situations, the veneer will partially cover the edge. It is nearly impossible to slip the edge material under the veneer once the veneer has been glued down. When choosing the proper edge for a specific project, there are two main considerations: the visual impact and the functional impact.

In most cases, the edge will need to be covered up so the core material is not visible. A related visual consideration is deciding whether you want to create the illusion of a solid board or whether you want the panel to have some sort of border or frame.

The second consideration is where and how the panel is to be used. Veneer is fairly durable as a surface covering where it doesn't see heavy use, such as on the middle of a table, on a shelf, and on most horizontal and vertical surfaces. Veneer becomes vulnerable on an edge where it can be bumped, scraped, or rubbed with daily use. Any time a veneered panel contacts the floor it will need additional protection because one scrape over the carpet or the floor can rip the veneer right off the surface. I usually apply a solid wood edge to protect these areas.

The author applied Macassar ebony veneer to the curved edge on this sideboard. The complete sideboard appears on page viii.

Figure 7-1. The solid wood edge on this veneered panel was applied first, before the face veneer. This way, the veneer can cover the edging with a joint that is almost invisible.

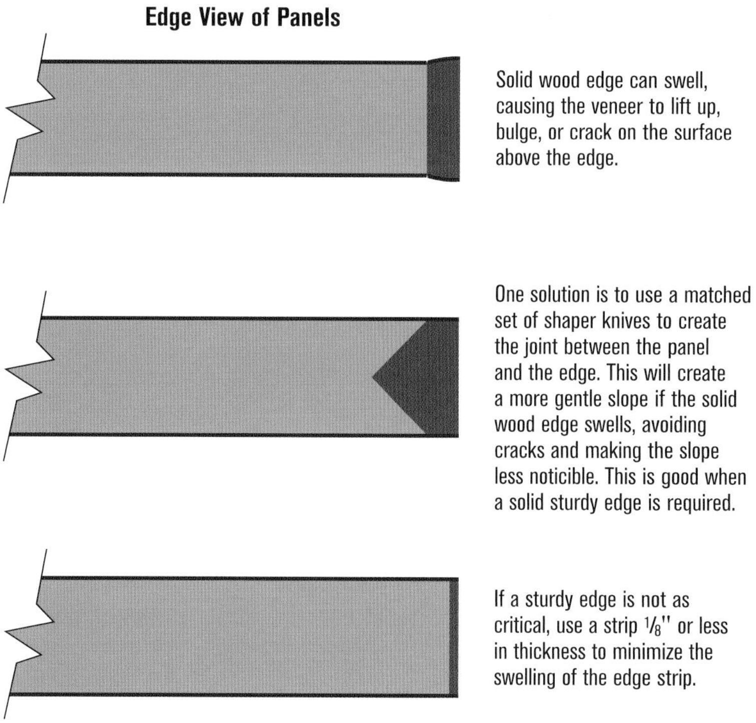

Edge View of Panels

Solid wood edge can swell, causing the veneer to lift up, bulge, or crack on the surface above the edge.

One solution is to use a matched set of shaper knives to create the joint between the panel and the edge. This will create a more gentle slope if the solid wood edge swells, avoiding cracks and making the slope less noticible. This is good when a solid sturdy edge is required.

If a sturdy edge is not as critical, use a strip 1/8" or less in thickness to minimize the swelling of the edge strip.

Figure 7-2. A solid wood edge that is applied and then veneered over creates a neat finished appearance, but it also may cause problems.

Solid wood edge

You can create the illusion of a solid board by attaching a solid wood edge to the substrate then veneering over it (**Figure 7-1**). There are several ways to accomplish it. In **Figure 7-2**, the edge material is first attached to the substrate before the veneer is applied. The complementary approach is to attach the solid wood edge after veneering the top surface, as will be shown in the step-by-step procedure on page 81.

When applying a wood edge before the surface veneer, the wood must be absolutely flush with the surface of the substrate because any unevenness will telegraph through the veneer. You can reach that goal using the router jig, a belt sander, or a hand plane. You must also consider the fact that any wood edge may swell or shrink a little relative to the substrate, which can cause the veneer to crack where the two join. A plain wooden edge of 1/8" to 1/4" in thickness will probably not move enough to cause a problem. If you want a wider border for a profiled edge, you might consider using a tapered tongue-and-groove bit when applying the edge, instead of biscuits or a spline. There may still be movement where the two pieces meet, but the seam will have a gentle and unnoticeable slope, instead of a crack in the veneer.

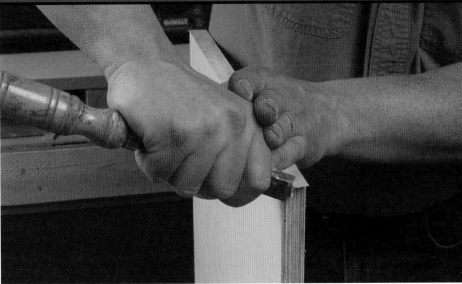

Figure 7-3. Cut the veneer tape to length, and iron it onto the edge of the substrate.

Figure 7-4. Press the veneer tape down with the veneer hammer, then trim it with a sharp chisel.

Veneer tape

Another way to create the illusion of a solid board on a panel that will not be in a high traffic area, for a horizontal application or on a curve, is to apply veneer directly to the edge of the panel after the surface veneer has been applied. The most common method is to use iron-on veneer tape, available at most lumberyards. It is available in ¾" widths in a few widely used species such as birch, maple, oak, and mahogany. It can also be obtained in a few species in 1" widths. It is good for edging veneered plywood on shelves and other projects of common woods, where an exact match is not required.

To apply veneer tape, place it over the edge to be covered (**Figure 7-3**), iron it down with a warm iron, and then apply a little pressure with a veneer hammer or like object. Trim the edge tape with a sharp chisel (**Figure 7-4**) and sand for finishing (**Figure 7-5**). There also are various tools, both ready-made and shop-made, for quicker application.

A painted edge is another nice option. However, the edge to be painted still must be covered with veneer to prevent the lines between the layers of the substrate from telegraphing through to the surface.

Figure 7-5. Once you have pressed and trimmed the tape, it's ready to sand.

Figure 7-6. To hammer veneer the edge, apply glue to the veneer and to the substrate and press the edge veneer into the glue.

Figure 7-7. Iron the veneer onto the edge and press it down tight with the veneer hammer.

Veneered edge

To match surface veneer exactly, the edge can be hammer-veneered using veneer from the same flitch as the surface veneer, as shown in **Figure 7-6**. You can glue the matching veneer to the substrate with either hide glue or PVA glue, as shown in **Figure 7-7** and detailed in Chapter 6.

Normally I apply the surface veneer first, then the edge veneer. On a fine piece, you might want to minimize line marking on the edge veneer by applying the edge veneer first. There is always the risk of damaging edge veneer or the end grain of the surface veneer. One solution is to cover the completed edge with blue painter's tape before

applying the surface veneer. Once the panel has been removed from the press, the tape can be removed, taking excess glue with it.

You often see a veneered top veneered with the same material, but with the grain of the edge veneer running up and down rather than flowing around the top, as shown in the opening photo for Chapter 7. It's not difficult to do, though you do have to crosscut a lot of short strips and lay them up with tape. It may be simplest to apply the edging before the surface.

Contrasting border

Another way to approach the design of a panel's edge is to visually separate it from the field in the center with a contrasting border or frame. The method, often used for tabletops, can create very durable visually stunning designs. In most cases, the veneer is applied to the panel before the border. Once the glue has cured, the panel can be trimmed to size and the border applied.

Layers of veneer also can be applied on edge, between the panel and the frame, to create the decorative detail shown in **Figure 7-8**. When applying a border, make sure it is slightly thicker than the panel so it can be sanded flush with the surface veneer. The surface veneer does not allow for any dimensional sanding if it ends up above the top surface of the border.

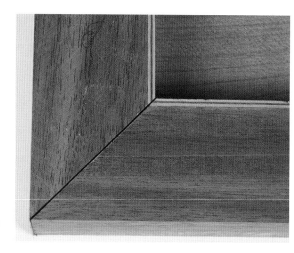

Figure 7-8. The light-dark-light band between the walnut edge and the panel is made of three strips of veneer, glued to the solid wood edging.

For the demonstration tabletop, I decided to construct a solid wood border around the outside edge, to protect it from wear and tear. I also like the idea of using a contrasting wood to help unify the design with the contrasting woods that make up the veneered panel (Figure 7-8). So in this case, I will glue the veneer to the panel first and then create and apply the border.

I usually make my panels about 1" oversize, so I can square them up and trim them to precise size later. Doing so allows room to square the panel up after gluing because the veneer can slide around during the gluing process. Also, because the

edge of a veneered panel is always the vulnerable area during construction, trimming the waste will remove all the little nicks and dents.

The solid wood edging must be thicker than the veneered panel, and it can be considerably thicker. In this example, I prepared 1¼"-square sectioned strips of walnut. Then, I faced one edge of the walnut with a three-veneer composite band, mitered its corners, and joined it to the veneered panel. The steps in making the solid wood edge are detailed below.

Step 1. Lay out the three veneer bands by tracing around the walnut edge pieces.

Step 2. Roll glue onto the three veneers as well as onto the edge piece, and tape the veneers in place. Clamp two of these assemblies together veneer to veneer, with a layer of wax paper between the two veneer stacks, so the glue can cure.

Step 3. Saw and then sand or plane the banding veneers flush with the walnut edge pieces.

Step 4. Miter the edge pieces so they will fit neatly around the veneered panel.

Step 5. Make biscuit slots to join the edging to the panel. Offset the slots by a single veneer thickness—just enough to make the edging stand proud of the veneered surface.

Step 6. Glue and clamp the solid wood edge to the veneered panel. When the clamps come off, plane and sand the edge flush with the veneer surface.

CHAPTER 8

Problems, Repairs & Finishing

At first glance, veneer can seem too fragile and unyielding a material with which to work. When properly considered, however, veneer's unique characteristics make it a durable and versatile material. It can be changed, flattened, repaired, or altered before it is applied to a surface or long after it has been glued down, and finished with relative ease. To understand the problems of veneer and make the most of the qualities that make it so versatile, remember wood is an organic and dynamic material that continues to react to its environment long after the tree has been cut.

If a sheet of veneer seems too lumpy or wrinkled to work with, the likely cause is uneven wood shrinkage during drying due to variations in the wood's grain structure and orientation. The solution is as simple as soaking the veneer in a chemical mix that can be absorbed into the cells of the veneer, allowing it to become pliable enough to be flattened. Veneer also is easy to cut, which makes patching with similar or contrasting materials relatively easy. Finally, a good understanding of the characteristics of the adhesives discussed in Chapter 5 will aid in repairing antique and contemporary pieces of furniture with damaged veneer.

To flatten gnarly veneers, soak them in a glue-based solution, then press them between sheets of clean newsprint.

Evaluating veneer problems

It is inevitable that some newly purchased veneers will arrive in less than usable condition. The condition usually is not the fault of the veneer supplier. There are several common problems associated with raw veneer that can, if treated properly, be corrected. Many types of burl and highly figured veneers will arrive in a very lumpy or wrinkled state, as shown in **Figure 8-1**. The highly variable grain structure in the veneers is what makes them so interesting and beautiful and, at the same time, difficult to use.

Most veneer logs are steamed before they are sliced into veneer, which relaxes the wood fibers and allows each sheet to be cut off more easily. After slicing, each sheet of veneer is laid flat and put through a dryer. Most straight-grained and many figured veneers will remain very flat after the process is completed because cells in the wood fibers release their moisture in a relatively uniform manner. Contraction and shrinking remain relatively uniform across the sheet. Burl and highly figured woods, however, have grain that travels in many directions. As the sheet

Veneer Flattening T E R M S

Dry-glue defects. Voids or bubbles under veneer caused by too little glue or improper adhesion are dry-glue defects. Remedy by adding new glue and pressing the defect flat.

Sizing. Sizing means filling the pores of the veneer with a water-soluble chemical mixture, typically including glycerin or an adhesive, to help keep it flat.

Veneer punch. A sharp cutting tool, or veneer punch, removes a circle or an irregular shape from veneer in order to cut out a small defect and make way for a patch cut with the same tool.

Wet-glue defects. Bulges in glued veneer caused by too much glue, called wet-glue defects, can be remedied by forcing excess glue out of the veneer.

dries, it shrinks at different rates, causing some areas to buckle and other areas to bulge. With such movement, it's a wonder some of the woods yield any usable veneer at all.

When you do receive lumpy and wrinkled burl or figured veneers, any attempt to flatten them with pressure alone will inevitably result in large cracks appearing over the entire surface. There are several good methods for flattening wrinkled veneers. Each method requires softening the wood fibers in the veneer, pressing the veneer flat, and keeping it flat, while allowing it to dry. Softening can be done using moisture, chemicals, heat, or some combination. Pressure can be applied with an iron, with clamps, with weights, or in a press. Whatever the method, moisture always must be removed gradually.

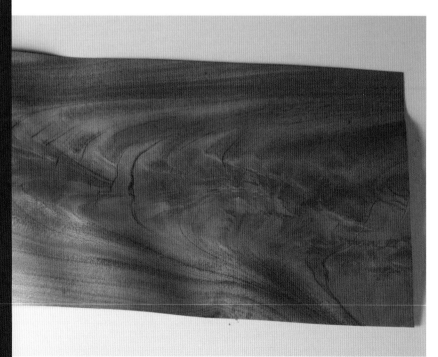

Figure 8-1. This wrinkled leaf of mahogany crotch veneer has spectacular feather figure but is also full of stresses. If it were simply pressed flat, it would crack in a dozen places.

Ironing veneer flat

The simplest method for flattening slightly wrinkled veneer is to moisten it with distilled water and iron it, just like a shirt, as shown in **Figures 8-2** and **8-3**. The method will not work if the sheet is deeply wrinkled or curled. I use an iron set to a medium heat with the steam function turned off. To wet the veneer, I use a spray bottle containing distilled water. I like to use a spray bottle instead of the steam iron because it gives me control of exactly where and when the moisture is applied. Use distilled water because additives in tap water and minerals in well water will stain the veneer, which is especially risky with delicately toned woods such as Swiss pear and holly. The problem is made worse when steam from the evaporating moisture forces impurities deep into the wood structure.

As the veneer flattens out, you can increase the pressure on the iron and also add more water to stubborn areas. Once the veneer seems flat, flip it over and iron the back to make sure all of the moisture is gone. Any moisture that remains after ironing will encourage the veneer to revert back to its original shape. You also can place the veneer between sheets of newsprint and put it in the veneer press to dry.

The ironing process can be improved by adding glycerin and alcohol to the water. Before adding any chemicals to the water, however, apply them to a scrap piece of veneer to make sure they will not stain it.

Figure 8-2. Many veneers can be flattened with moisture and heat. Try spritzing a sample with distilled water on both sides of the leaf.

Figure 8-3. Set the iron to medium heat with the steam function turned off, and press the dampened veneer flat. Start with light pressure and gradually increase it.

Sizing the veneer

Seriously wrinkled veneers can be prepared for flattening by sizing them with water and a chemical mixture. Sizing generally begins by softening the veneer with glycerin and then filling the wood cells with something to hold them in place, typically a type of adhesive. Following application, leave the veneer to dry under pressure to hold its new flat shape. An iron generally is not used here.

Figure 8-4. A paint brush is a good applicator for sizing solution. Brush the material liberally onto both sides of the veneer leaf.

There are several formulas listed below. All are applied in a similar manner. The veneer is first thoroughly soaked with the mixture (**Figure 8-4**). Then, several leaves are stacked together like a sandwich, with at least two pieces of clean inkless newsprint between each leaf, as shown in the step-by-step sequence. The stack is then placed between two sheets of plywood or MDF, and pressure is applied with weights, clamps, or a veneer press. The newsprint will need to be changed every hour at first, then less frequently as the veneer begins to dry. The entire drying process takes one or two days. It's very important

to allow the veneer to dry completely before laying it up and gluing it down. Also, it is a good idea to use the newly flattened veneer as quickly as possible; otherwise, it's liable to wrinkle again. If it has to be stored, keep it pressed flat, but inspect it often and occasionally change the newsprint to keep mildew from forming.

To allow the moisture to escape a little faster, place plastic window screens between the layers of newsprint and the wet veneer before pressing. The screen also will allow you to use old newspapers instead of clean newsprint because it prevents the ink on the newspaper from touching the veneer. Be careful not to apply too much pressure because the screen can emboss the surface of the veneer. Corrugated cardboard with the ridges facing the veneer is another option for a material to place between the sheets of veneer—it increases the amount of air that passes through the stack.

Sizing mixtures

You can buy a mixture formulated for flattening veneers. ProGlue veneer softener is one such, and it works quite well. You also can mix your own. The formulas for softening veneer have a variety of components. Some formulas include glue, which helps to stabilize the veneer after it dries. Most formulas are quite similar to the traditional formula I first learned from the late Tage Frid at Rhode Island School of Design (**Figure 8-5**). This formula consists of:

- two parts powdered glue (Frid used cascamite, which is now difficult to find, so I use urea formaldehyde),
- one part flour (as a filler),
- one-and-one-half parts glycerin (for softening),
- one part alcohol (which aids in moisture penetration, speeds drying and reduces mildew growth),
- three parts distilled water.

Mix the dry ingredients, and then slowly add the distilled water, mixing well (**Figure 8-6**). Finally, add the alcohol and glycerin, and stir them in well. Paint the mixture onto both sides of the veneer, or, in the case of small leaves of burl, pour the mixture into a shallow pan and soak the veneer in it. Then, dry the veneers between sheets of clean newsprint, as discussed above. When adding glue to any formula, make sure the adhesive you plan to use later to fasten the veneer to the substrate will be compatible with the adhesive in the sizing formula.

A variation of the sizing formula consists of:

- two parts white PVA glue,
- one part glycerin,
- one part alcohol,
- three to four parts water.

You can experiment with different adhesives and softening agents depending on the particular veneers you are trying to flatten, but keep in mind what residues will be left behind and how these residues may affect both the gluing and the finishing process. There are several types of commercially available veneer softeners, which also work very well. They have the advantage of being ready to use.

Hide glue also can be used to flatten veneer. The veneer is first soaked with hide glue and then applied to the substrate, which has had a coat of hide glue applied to it as well. While the hide glue is still wet, the veneer is first heated with an iron and then flattened out and pressed down with a veneer hammer. This process will flatten the veneer and bond it to the substrate at the same time.

Figure 8-5. The ingredients for the sizing formula are white flour, powdered plastic resin glue, glycerin, methyl alcohol, and distilled water.

Figure 8-6. Mix the dry ingredients, then add the liquids. Stir well to eliminate lumps.

Wrinkled and buckled veneers must be flattened before they can be laid up and pressed onto a panel. I've had success using a glycerin-based sizing mixture to fill the pores, and then I press the veneers flat while they dry. Here's the technique:

Step 1. Spread the sizing mixture on all the leaves of veneer. Cover the bench with newspaper to contain the mess.

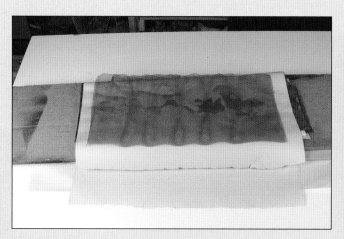

Step 2. Stack the veneers between sheets of newsprint and layers of fiberglass window screen. The screen helps the moisture escape.

Step 3. Load the stack into the veneer press and apply light pressure. Let it dry there for an hour. Then, remove the stack, change the paper, and press again. Repeat this process several times.

Step 4. Remove the stack from the press, change the newsprint, remove the screening, and replace the veneers in the press with increased pressure overnight.

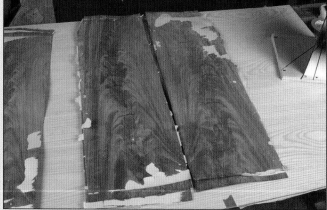

Step 5. The sizing material fills the cracks and pores in the wood, allowing it to flatten out with no cracks. Bits of newsprint are likely to stick to the veneers. It has to be scraped off before you can glue the veneer to a substrate.

Patching defects

Raw veneer may contain holes, knots, and small cracks, which can be patched before it is applied to a surface. Your first option might be to return the veneers to the supplier, but because most suppliers do not charge for defective areas, you might want to patch it and use it anyway. A small defect can significantly lower the price of an expensive and beautiful sheet of veneer. Also, veneer easily can be damaged in the shop—you won't be able to return it, but you can always patch it.

Veneer patches can either be hidden in the wood figure or become a decorative element on the surface. The butterfly details in George Nakashima's solid wood benches and tabletops are a good example of a surface repair that evolved into a personal decorative motif. There are several methods for setting veneer patches into a sheet of veneer before it is applied to a substrate. The patch can be inlaid using a knife, employing the process of inlaying described in Chapter 9. As discussed, always work from the back of the sheet. Another way to apply a patch is to use the techniques of marquetry. Both approaches allow you to follow the wood grain when cutting out the area to be replaced with a veneer patch. Done carefully, either process can make a defect all but invisible.

The veneer punch, shown in **Figure 8-7**, is another traditional method for cutting out a defect and replacing it with sound veneer. Veneer punches are sold in a variety of sizes, and in various free-form shapes, with the circle and the kidney-bean shape the most common. The punch works on the same principle as the double cut method of marquetry. The punch will cut out a bevel-sided hole and a bevel-edged piece of veneer to place in it at the same time. Punches can be expensive, but a shop-made punch, formed from a short length of electrical conduit, can work nearly as well.

Figure 8-7. The veneer punch can be used to remove the damaged spot from a leaf of veneer, and also to cut a perfectly fitting patch from another veneer.

To make a veneer punch, start with a length of electrical conduit or some other relatively soft metal pipe. Shape the end with a hammer, pliers, or blacksmithing tools as shown in the step-by-step sequence on page 90. To soften the metal, add heat. Once shaped, grind it sharp. The angle should be around 30 degrees. Next, clean up any burrs with a file, and go back over the cutting edge with a sharp file. The finished punch is shown in Step 4.

You'll have best results with the punch if you experiment a bit first. For the best fitting patch, punch the veneer to be repaired from one side, and the repair veneer from the other side. This way, the bevels made by the punch will complement one another, and the patch will fit perfectly on the face side of the veneer. Put blue tape on the side of the veneer opposite the punch to help prevent unwanted cracking. With the patch in place, tape over the face side using paper veneer tape.

Veneer punches, used to remove a damaged spot in the veneer and replace it with a little patch of sound material, are difficult to find and quite expensive. But you can make your own from a short piece of thin-walled tubing, such as electrical conduit. Here's how:

Step 1. Hammer the end of the electrical conduit to make it oval shaped or bean shaped. You can also squeeze it in the bench vise.

Step 2. Grind the end of the shaped conduit to make it sharp. Extend the bevel ⅛" or more up the conduit.

Step 3. File the inside of the punch to remove the burr and make its edge as sharp as possible.

Step 4. Here's the completed punch, alongside the kind of veneer defect it can repair.

Step 5. Put blue tape on the back of the defect; then, punch it through from the face side.

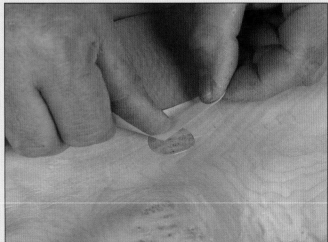

Step 6. Press the patch into place and secure it with paper veneer tape on the face side. In this example, I replaced the tear in the veneer with a burly patch.

Repairs after gluing up

Defects that appear after the veneer has been glued down can be repaired. A good understanding of how to repair such defects will prevent many of them from reappearing after new work has left the shop. Also, the ability to repair various defects in older work may seem mysterious and difficult at first, but it actually is not as complicated as it seems. Being ready and able to do repairs can be a good source of extra income.

The best time to identify and repair the most common defects is immediately after removing the panel from the veneer press. Defects will appear as blisters, wrinkles, or other raised areas in the veneer. The defects fall into two categories: wet-glue defects and dry-glue defects.

Wet-glue defects need to be repaired right away, before the glue hardens. Wet-glue defects are caused by either too much glue or not enough clamping pressure.

Dry-glue defects are loose spots caused by too little glue or too much pressure. It is best to wait a day or two until the glue has fully cured before repairing dry-glue defects. To distinguish between the two, tap on any raised areas with your fingernail, as shown in **Figure 8-8**. If you hear a hollow sound, there is a dry-glue problem. If the tapping sounds solid, there is wet glue under the surface, and it needs to be dealt with right away.

Wet-Glue Defects

Wet-glue defects are easiest to repair if PVA glue was used, although it is possible to repair them to some extent when other glues were used. Severe wet-glue problems may send the entire panel to the garbage can. There are two things that need to happen if a repair is to succeed. First, the excess glue needs to be removed from the area. Second, pressure needs to be applied in order to flatten the veneer while the remaining glue dries. If the wrinkle is near the edge of the panel, the excess glue can be forced out to the edge with a veneer hammer. Glue can actually be forced from quite a distance to the edge if there is a path the glue can follow. If the wrinkle is enclosed or if it is near the center of the panel, make a small knife-cut along the grain at one corner of the bubble and use the veneer hammer to force the glue out through it (**Figure 8-9**).

After forcing out the excess glue, the veneer needs to be flattened, which ultimately determines whether or not the panel can be saved. If there is a large bubble or wrinkle surrounded by correctly bonded veneer, when you flatten the bubble, the excess veneer needs somewhere to go. If the defect is near the edge, the excess veneer can be worked out to the edge. If the defect is small and surrounded by glued-down veneer, the pressure of reclamping the bubble will force the fibers closer together.

Figure 8-8. When a panel first comes out of the press, you'll be able to feel any bubbles or ripples in the surface. Tapping them with a fingernail will confirm whether they are dry and not glued, or wet and containing a thick patch of glue.

Figure 8-9. Slit the wet-glue defect. Use the iron and the veneer hammer to force the excess glue out.

If forcing out the glue and flattening the bubble causes a ridge or wave to appear, make a knife cut through the ridge to relieve the pressure and to allow the excess veneer to overlap itself. Once flattened, make a knife cut though both layers of veneer in order to remove the excess veneer and create a seam that can be taped before applying pressure. To help to hide to seam, make sure to tilt the knife to create an angled cut.

Another method is to iron out the defect with a warm iron and flatten it with a veneer hammer, following the techniques detailed in Chapter 6. If using PVA glue, the process will set the glue and help to shrink the veneer right where the excess needs to be removed. Heating too large an area risks softening the glue in properly bonded areas. You might also shrink the veneer too much, causing a knife cut to open.

Repairing Wet-Glue Defects

Wet-glue defects need to be repaired immediately, before the glue hardens. Here are the steps you need to take:

Step 1. Determine if the glue is enclosed or can be forced out an edge.

Step 2. Slit the defect with a small knife if it is enclosed or near the center of the panel. If the defect is near the edge, move on to Step 3.

Step 3. Use an iron and a veneer hammer to force the excess glue out. If a ridge appears, cut through it to relieve the pressure. Allow the excess veneer to overlap. Once the area is flat, remove the excess veneer with a knife to create a seam. Tilt the knife to angle the cut and help hide the seam. Tape the seam.

Step 4. Apply pressure to flatten the veneer while the remaining glue dries.

Dry-Glue Defects

Most defects are dry-glue problems caused either by too little glue or too much clamp pressure. Dry-glue defects appear as loose spots, bubbles, or wrinkles and are generally easy to repair no matter what type of glue was used, although they do need to wait until after the original glue has been allowed to set completely. New loose spots also can appear as the panel is being cleaned.

There are several reasons for loose spots, which are actually small areas of the veneer that did not properly adhere to the substrate. The first and most common cause is unequal spreading of the adhesive. There may not have been enough glue to bond the veneer in some small area. The second most common reason for loose spots is an overall lack of adhesive. What seems like enough glue for a non-porous veneer such as hard maple and a non-porous substrate such as MDF won't be enough glue for more porous veneers such as mahogany applied to a lauan substrate. The glue may soak into the wood grain and disappear. When initially gluing porous woods, I allow the first coat of glue to soak in for a minute or two before applying another thin coat of glue to the substrate. Adding a little extra glue around the edges of the panel before laying the veneer also can prevent loose veneer there. The third cause for loose spots is too much clamp pressure. Too much pressure can force the glue deep into the wood fibers, leaving too little on the surface to make a good join.

Cleaning and sanding veneered panels

Once you have glued up a veneered panel, you will need to remove the veneer tape, repair any defects, and scrape or sand the panel so it is ready for finishing. It is easiest to remove the veneer tape, make small repairs, clean up the panel with a scraper, and sand the surface all at the same time. In most cases, I like to get veneered panels sanded to the 220-grit stage before trimming them and incorporating them into a project. Doing so keeps the vulnerable edges of the veneer protected as long as possible and also allows each panel to be sanded to its final thickness before cutting any joints.

To remove the veneer tape, wet the tape along its length with a spray bottle or sponge. It does not take a lot of water, but there should be enough to soak through the tape. Allow the tape to soak for about five minutes. When the color of the tape has changed from white to gray, it is ready to be removed either by hand or by using a cabinet scraper with a burr (**Figure 8-10**).

The presence of moisture on the surface of the veneer from removal of the tape makes this a good time to go ahead and dampen the entire surface and check it for loose spots. Dampen both the front and the back of the panel at the same time, to prevent the panel from cupping due to non-uniform drying. The surface does not need to be flooded with distilled water, but the entire surface should be damp. A spray bottle or a damp rag will work well for applying a limited amount of water.

After spritzing the panel, place it where air can get at both sides. Allow it to dry for about 20 minutes. As the panel dries, any loose spots will spring up as bubbles or blisters. Tap the surface again with your finger and listen for hollow sounds to identify any new loose spots caused by the addition of the moisture. If you find any, circle them with pencil and proceed to the next steps.

Some craftsmen do not like exposing the entire veneered surface to water, but I find the benefits far outweigh any costs. It is far better to find defects now rather than after the piece has been sent out. Even after many coats of finish have been applied to the

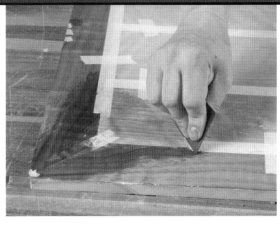

Figure 8-10. To remove the veneer tape, moisten it and scrape with a cabinet scraper. A spritz of distilled water won't harm the glued-up panel.

surface, moisture will get to the veneer sooner or later, either by water spilled on the surface or by humidity present in the environment. This will cause a loose spot to bubble up just as described above, unless you cause the reaction in your shop and repair it first.

If you plan to use a water-based finish, it is always a good idea to raise the grain with water and then sand it down before applying the finish. Cleaning and sanding the panel now will take the place of that step. Also, when a water-based finish is applied, the surface will, in effect, become flooded with water. If being wet will damage it, finishing will cause the same damage. I often finish my work with various types of lacquers, and I have had no problems with this procedure. If a shellac-based finish is to be applied, consider using alcohol to wet the surface. If oil-based polyurethane is to be used, paint thinner can be used to wet the surface.

To sand a veneered panel, use a random orbit sander with 220-grit sandpaper. When I start with 220 grit, I rarely sand through the veneer. If I am using a very soft or thin veneer, I will hand-sand the panel. You may want to begin by hand sanding all of your veneer work instead of using a sander, until you get used to working with veneer. A good way to test the sanding properties of any veneer is to glue up a sample board and try to sand it using various techniques.

Repairing loose spots

To repair loose spots, you have to get new glue under the surface and then apply pressure to the affected area. The first consideration is the type of glue to be used. There might already be a small amount of glue under the loose spots. If so, the old glue must bond with whatever glue you are using to fix that area. I usually assume that if there wasn't enough glue to bond the veneer to the substrate, there probably isn't enough glue to interfere with the repair. That is not always the case, however, so there are some precautions that can be taken. When white or yellow glues were used to bond the veneer to the substrate, the area to be repaired can be slightly heated to loosen any glue present. The glue will then dry under pressure with any new white or yellow glue applied to the defect. Keep the heat right on the affected area to prevent softening the properly bonded areas around the defect. When other glues were used, and you suspect there might be enough to be troublesome, you may want to use epoxy to repair the defect. It can be messy, but it will stick to almost anything.

Figure 8-11. When you find a loose spot under the veneer, carefully slit it with the knife. Try to slit one edge of the spot, and hold the knife at an angle leaning away from the spot.

Slit the Bubble

After selecting the proper glue, there are various methods for getting it under the surface of the veneer (**Figure 8-11**). The process is analogous to performing surgery.

The procedure begins by opening the wound with an incision along the length of one side of the bubble, following the grain. Use a sharp breakaway knife, a craft knife or a scalpel tilted to the left, away from the defect at a very sharp angle of 10 to 15 degrees off the face of the panel. The sharp angle will minimize the appearance of the cut later, and there will be enough surface on the faces of the cut to bond the veneer back together. Follow the grain as closely as possible so the cut will appear to be part of the grain. If there is a dark line in the wood figure where you want to make the cut, follow it with the knife. The dark line also will help in hiding the glue line.

Force Glue Under the Veneer

Now that the defect has been opened up, glue needs to be forced into the entire area that is loose. You can use a glue injector to inject glue under the surface. The injector can be inserted through the cut, and glue can then be applied to all areas of the defect. If you don't have an injector, or if you don't want the hassle of cleaning it up after each use, the glue can be applied manually. With the knife still in the cut and the blade pointing away from the center, twist the knife slightly to open up a slot. Place a small bead of glue along the length of the opening and use a veneer scrap, a palette knife, or a brush to push the glue into the opening, moving perpendicular to the cut (**Figure 8-12**). When the glue disappears, add another bead of glue and repeat the process. Each new bead of glue forces the previous glue farther back into the defect. Keep repeating the process until the new glue will not disappear.

Be careful using a strip of sturdy, straight-grained veneer to force the glue even farther back into the defect—you do not want the veneer strip to break off inside the defect. Because this procedure is started from one side of the defect, you should be able to get glue under the entire loose area. However, do not attempt to turn the knife over the other way in an attempt to force glue back under the other side of the cut. Doing so will tear up the veneer around the cut, making it all but impossible to conceal. If it looks like more glue needs to be placed, in this case, to the right of the knife, make another cut farther to the right and repeat this procedure again. If the area looks too large to repair all at once, go on to the pressing procedure and come back to repeat this process after the glue has set. Once the glue has been applied, push the bubble down by hand to squeeze the excess glue out through the cut. Wipe away the excess glue with a damp paper towel to reduce scraping and sanding later.

Press the Bubble Flat

Now you are ready to apply pressure to the defect. The repaired defect can be ironed down with an iron and a veneer hammer (**Figure 8-13**). Ironing can work very well when hide glue was initially used to glue down the veneer but can cause two problems. First, it is difficult to keep the heat right on the defect. Heat around the edges of the defect can loosen more veneer, causing an ever-bigger loose spot to form. Second, veneer can shrink when it is heated and dried, perhaps opening up the knife cut.

The best solution is to get pressure right on the spot that needs it. One way is to put the entire panel back into the vacuum bag or the veneer press. Pressure also can be applied directly to the defect using clamps and curved cauls or bowed boards placed with their crowns right over the defect. When the boards are clamped from the ends, the curve applies pressure directly to the spot that needs it. You also can use two straight boards with a small ¼"-thick piece of wood placed over the spot. Either way, place a piece of

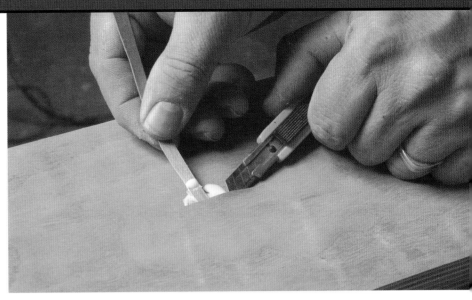

Figure 8-12. Hold the slit open with the knife blade while you use a scrap of veneer to push glue into it. Push the glue everywhere you can reach.

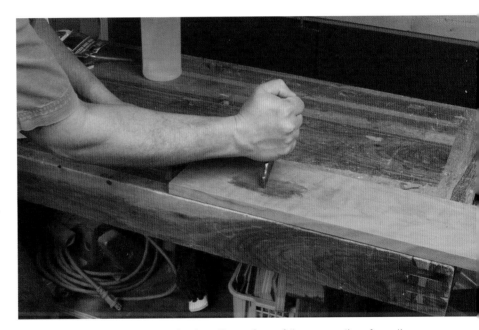

Figure 8-13. Wipe the excess glue from the surface of the veneer, then force the repair flat with the veneer hammer.

wax paper or newsprint over the glue line to prevent the glue from bonding the board to the surface. An additional method for pressing down a small area of veneer in the center of a panel without clamps is simply to apply a heavy weight to a board placed right over the area to be pressed.

Before sanding, any excess glue around the patch will need to be removed with a cabinet scraper. Now is a good time to scrape off any dried glue from the panel's entire surface to

Repairing Dry-Glue Defects

Dry-glue defects must be repaired once the glue has set. Here is the basic method:

Step 1. Dampen the entire surface with a liquid appropriate for the finish you'll use. Dampen both the front and the back at the same time to prevent any cupping due to non-uniform drying. Do not flood the surface. A spray bottle or a damp rag works well for applying a limited amount of water. Check the panel for loose spots by tapping your finger on the surface.

Step 2. Place the panel where air can reach both sides. Allow it to dry for about 20 minutes. Tap the surface again and listen for hollow sounds to identify any new loose spots caused by the addition of the moisture. Circle any you find with pencil.

Step 3. Select the proper glue. The old glue must bond with whatever glue you are using to fix that area.

Step 4. Tilt a sharp knife to the left, away from the defect, at a very sharp angle of 10 to 15 degrees off the face of the panel. The angle minimizes the appearance of the cut and may help hide the glue line. Slit the bubble by cutting along the length of one side, following the grain.

Step 5. Force glue into the loose area using a glue injector; alternatively, place a small bead of glue along the length of the opening and use a veneer scrap, palette knife, or brush to push the glue into the opening. Repeat the process until the new glue will not disappear. If you use a veneer strip, do not break it off inside the defect.

Step 6. Once the glue has been applied, push the bubble down by hand to squeeze out the excess glue. Wipe away excess glue with a damp paper towel.

Step 7. Iron the defect with an iron and a veneer hammer, put the entire panel back into the vacuum bag or the veneer press, or apply pressure directly to the defect using clamps and curved cauls or bowed boards placed with their crowns right over the defect.

Step 8. Remove any excess glue around the patch with a cabinet scraper to prepare for sanding.

prepare it for sanding. Scraping is the best method for removing dried glue. Sandpaper will remove the soft veneer around the hardened glue much faster than it removes the glue itself, forming a low spot. It is possible to sand right through the veneer before removing all the glue. Be careful to scrape in a direction that does not tear out or raise the grain, perhaps diagonally. It may be hard to tell when the glue is gone, but if you don't get it all, the remaining glue may show up as a spot when you apply a finish. To make sure all of the glue has been removed, examine the shavings closely while scraping. The scrapings containing glue will have a different color, usually lighter. Once all of the scrapings show the same color and texture, all of the glue has been removed and the panel is ready for sanding.

Veneer finishing

The process of finishing a veneered surface is quite similar to the process of a finishing a solid wood surface. Some finishes, however, are not as effective on veneer, notably penetrating oil finishes. Penetrating oils need to sink deep into the surface of the wood to be effective. Products such as Watco Danish Oil Finish will absorb into the wood fibers and bond them together to a depth of $\frac{1}{16}$" to $\frac{1}{8}$". On a veneered panel, such finishes cannot penetrate past the glue line bonding the veneer to the substrate, so they do not get deep enough to work properly.

Non-penetrating finishes, including lacquer, varnish, and shellac, work very well on veneered surfaces. A finish for veneer needs to be hard enough to protect the surface of the wood on its own. Varnish and shellac can be applied with a brush. Lacquer needs to be sprayed.

Earlier in the book, I mentioned sanding the veneered panel, starting and ending with 220-grit sandpaper, before fitting it into any type of frame. After the piece has been assembled, and just prior to applying the finish, I sand everything with 320-grit sandpaper. I may

Figure 8-14. An HVLP spray unit makes it possible to spray lacquer in the small shop or outdoors nearby.

proceed to additional sanding with finer grits during the finishing process, depending on the type of finish I am working with and the amount of sheen desired.

I prefer to apply some type of lacquer to my veneered pieces. All types of lacquer will work well, including nitrocellulose, pre-catalyzed, and water-based, which are the industry standards and are relatively easy to apply. Lacquers hold up well to everyday use, withstand constant cleaning and polishing with most commercially available products and can be repaired. I apply lacquer with a spray gun, preferring a high-pressure-low-volume (HVLP) sprayer in a spray booth. I also have had very good luck spraying outside, as shown in **Figure 8-14**. One very effective finish that combines the characteristics of penetrating finishes and hard finishes is a shop-mixed varnish and oil finish. The mixture is excellent on pieces that combine solid wood and veneered surfaces and doesn't require any special equipment to apply. To create a basic recipe, combine ⅓ Danish, tung, or linseed oil with ⅓ turpentine and ⅓ oil-based varnish. (The formula is also available from various manufacturers in a pre-mixed form.) The finish is brushed on, allowed to soak in, and then wiped off before it becomes sticky. I apply at least four coats, allowing each one to dry overnight.

Repairing finished work

The most common types of damage to older veneered surfaces are blistering, much like the dry defects discussed above, and large areas of loose veneer or missing pieces of veneer. When a piece of furniture of unknown origin arrives in the shop, there are several things to check before beginning any repair. Start by determining if all of the veneer to make the repair is present. If so, what type of adhesive was used to hold down the veneer? It's always best to use the same kind of glue to make the repair.

Hide glue was used to build many older pieces. To determine if hide glue was used in the original construction, place a small piece of wet paper towel or the corner of a wet rag in an inconspicuous area of the panel or on the edge of the defect. Next, heat a small spot through the damp rag with the tip of a warm iron. If the veneer loosens easily and produces a foul smell, that's hide glue.

With hide glue, blisters can be repaired using the following procedure. First, place a damp cloth over the blister. Apply heat with a warm iron, and then apply pressure. The pressure can be applied with the iron itself, with a veneer hammer, with clamps and cauls, or by placing a heavy weight over the repaired area. If this procedure does not work, either there may not be enough glue present to affect a good repair, or the original glue was not hide glue and will not set with heat.

Repairing Blisters

If your project had hide glue, repair blisters using this procedure:

Step 1. Place a damp cloth over the blister.

Step 2. Apply heat with a warm iron.

Step 3. Apply pressure with the iron itself, with a veneer hammer, with clamps and cauls, or with a heavy weight on the repaired area.

Step 4. If the blister is not repaired by Steps 1 to 3, follow the directions on pages 94 and 95, using a knife to scrape any old glue from the substrate and from the underside of the veneer.

With other types of glue, follow the procedure described earlier in this chapter on repairing blisters in new work. Once the defect has been opened, use a knife to scrape any old, dried-up glue from the substrate and from the underside of the veneer. Frequently, the old glue has turned to dust and can be removed easily. These cleaned surfaces will allow you to use white or yellow glue to bond the veneer. New hide glue, either mixed from beads or the type that comes pre-mixed in a bottle, is also an excellent choice for repair work, even when you are not sure it was the original glue. Hide glue will stick to almost any surface, including those with another type of glue already present.

Loose Veneer

If large areas of veneer are loose, there are several options for repair. Large areas can easily be cleaned up and reglued as described above. If the entire surface is coming loose, the veneer can be scrapped and replaced, but, if possible, it is usually better to save it. If the veneer is to be saved, examine the substrate closely and determine if it caused the veneer to loosen and needs to be repaired or replaced.

Veneer has changed relatively little over the years, though new veneer may be thinner than older veneers. Glue, as we have seen, has changed a lot and may be replaced during a drastic repair. Substrates also have changed greatly. Many older pieces of furniture have veneer that was glued to some sort of solid wood substrate. While there were many attempts to construct them in a way that addressed movement of the solid wood under the veneer, the inevitable result was the veneer coming loose. A permanent solution would be to make an entirely new panel with a new substrate and replacement veneer. If the substrate cannot be replaced because it is part of the structure of the piece, the old veneer can be removed and replaced with new veneer. Or the old veneer can be carefully removed and reglued to a new substrate.

Removing Veneer from a Surface

The procedure described here works best for surfaces originally bonded with hide glue. In instances where it is necessary to remove veneer from a substrate, either to replace the veneer or the substrate, follow these steps:

Step 1. Strip off any finish and lightly sand the surface of the veneer.

Step 2. Place a wet towel or rag on the surface and allow moisture to soak in.

Step 3. Iron the surface with a household iron, forcing the heat and moisture deep into the surface.

Step 4. Use a wide putty knife or drywall knife to scrape off the entire sheet from underneath. Add more water and heat as needed.

Old veneer that was glued down with hide glue can be removed by first stripping off any finish and lightly sanding the surface. Lay a wet towel or rag on the surface and allow the moisture to soak in. Iron the surface with a household iron, forcing the heat and moisture deep into the surface. Use a wide putty knife or drywall knife to scrape off the entire sheet from underneath. Add more water and heat as needed.

Small Patches

If the surface to be repaired looks fairly good but has some small areas of veneer missing, these small areas can be patched. The operation usually involves refinishing the surface, so I like to go ahead and strip the finish off the surface and then sand it lightly. Refinishing will ensure the veneer selected for the patch will match the original veneer as closely as possible because the aging process will begin at the same time for the patch and the original veneer. The finish will be uniform throughout the piece.

Once the finish has been removed and the surface sanded, there are several methods for applying a patch. The first method is to secure the piece of veneer to be patched over the surface with painter's tape. Guide a knife with a straightedge or with a curved template and cut through both layers of veneer at the same time. Tilt the knife slightly away from the patch to create a wedge-shaped inlay. With a sharp chisel, remove the waste veneer and any excess glue from the surface. Next, apply glue to the patch and the substrate; then, tape the patch in place to keep it from shifting under pressure. Other methods for creating a small patch for the surface are using a router with an inlay jig or using a veneer punch.

Fixing Small Patches

Small areas of missing veneer can be patched, but the process does involve refinishing the surface. Here's the procedure:

Step 1. Strip off any finish and lightly sand the surface of the veneer.

Step 2. Secure the piece of veneer that is to be patched over the surface with painter's tape.

Step 3. Tilt the knife slightly away from the patch to create a wedge-shaped inlay. Guide a knife with a straightedge or with a curved template and cut through both layers of veneer at the same time.

Step 4. With a sharp chisel, remove the waste veneer and any excess glue from the surface.

Step 5. Apply glue to the patch and the substrate. Then, tape the patch in place to keep it from shifting under pressure.

When the demonstration tabletop panel came out of the veneer press, I carefully inspected the surface for bubbles and loose spots. Then, I spritzed the panel with distilled water and let it sit for a few minutes, until the paper veneer tape became soft and somewhat translucent. At that point, the tape could be pulled and scraped off the surface (as shown in the photo below).

While the panel was still wet, I carefully ran my fingers over the entire surface to look for loose spots. When you do this, tap any suspect spots with your fingernail. Repeat the inspection after it has dried. The moisture will expand any loose spots, making them easy to detect and repair. Once all of the bubbles and loose spots are fixed, sand the entire panel to 220-grit.

CHAPTER 9

Complex Matching, Inlays & Borders

Many veneer designs start with basic book matching. A radial match, for example, is created by book matching six to as many as twelve or even sixteen pie-shaped pieces of veneer. The circle can then be inlaid into a field of another type of veneer as shown in **Figure 9-15** and to the left. Burl veneers are often matched four ways, as shown in **Figure 9-14**, to create beautiful organic, yet formal, patterns. Many extremely interesting patterns and designs can be produced by combining techniques and processes, including inlaying both curved and straight-lined shapes and adding borders. Traditional marquetry and parquetry techniques also are useful and will be detailed in Chapter 10. After any design is taped together or laid up and prepared for gluing, it can be applied to a variety of flat or curved substrates.

Because most of these designs are based in part on book matching, it's important to get comfortable with the basic book-match first. Complex procedures fall into place quickly for most people once they master the basic two-sheet book-match. The jig and shooter techniques used in Chapter 3 to create tight seams are also used in this chapter, though some are slightly altered to create more complex patterns. By combining and experimenting with these techniques, you will be able to develop your own ideas and create truly unique designs.

Macassar ebony inlaid into curly maple makes the diamond match on this table leaf, which fits into a sunburst in the tabletop. The completed table can be seen at the start of Chapter 3 on page 24.

Figure 9-1. The six examples of four-way matches were all made using squares of Macassar ebony veneer.

Four-way match

Let's start with a few four-sheet, or four-way, matches and then progress to patterns that incorporate more sheets of veneer. By combining four sheets of the same straight-grained veneer, you can create at least six different types of matches. Woods with a strong linear grain pattern, such as Macassar ebony, are excellent for creating and illustrating these patterns (**Figure 9-1**). The six patterns were created using the same four leaves in different arrangements and with different cuts.

The diamond pattern and the X pattern on the left side of Figure 9-1 were created by cutting sheets in a square shape with the grain at a 45-degree angle to the cut. The cross and square diaper patterns in the center of Figure 9-1 were created by cutting triangular pieces of veneer with the grain at a 45-degree angle to the cut. On the right of Figure 9-1, on top, four identical squares are arranged to form a larger square, and below, two of the squares are matched with two diagonal pieces borrowed from the first match. The six examples do not exhaust the possibilities.

To preview how almost any type of match will look before actually cutting the veneer, make a jig that holds two mirrors at a variety of different angles, as shown in **Figures 9-2** and **9-3**. The jig can be moved over the surface of the veneer, letting you view many possible matches. The jig allows for the viewing of matches containing up to sixteen sheets of veneer. Once you have established where you want to make your cuts, just draw the line on the surface of the veneer using the edge of the mirror as a straightedge.

Veneer Matching T E R M S

Banding. Lines of veneer inlaid into a veneer field are called banding. Banding is normally taped to the field veneers before pressing.

Border. Veneers cut to fit around a central field are borders. Many veneered panels need a border to appear complete.

Field. The background veneer in a veneered panel with a border or inlay is called the field.

Four-way match. Four successive leaves of veneer arranged around a central point, with the wood figure reflected right to left and top to bottom, is known as a four-way match.

Kerf. The width of a saw cut, which in veneer work must be compensated for in some way, is called a kerf. When setting an inlay into a veneer field, sawing the opening would create a kerf and would require the inlay to be made correspondingly larger to fill the kerf.

Radial match. When triangles of identical veneer are fit together to make a circle, a radial match is made. A radial match commonly has 8, 12, or 16 veneer points.

One way to cut four-way matches is to tape the leaves into a tight bundle in flitch order and tape them into a sandwich between plates of thin plywood or MDF (**Figure 9-4**). Cut the package on the chop saw or on the table saw (**Figure 9-5**), using a sliding crosscut box. Once you have sawn one edge of the package, use the edge to reference subsequent cuts. After the first cuts, you can draw layout lines right on the MDF package.

A new problem arises with multiple sheet matches where the pattern repeats itself more than once before returning back to match the first sheet. As leaves of veneer are cut from deeper into a log, the grain pattern begins to shift. By the fourth leaf, the pattern will change enough that the grain will no longer perfectly match the first leaf. The pattern change can become a big problem when you try to match eight, ten, or even sixteen leaves. There is a simple solution: Mix up the order of the leaves a little, so there will only be a slight variation between any two. One way to do it is to number the consecutive leaves first (**Figure 9-6**) and then arrange them so no piece touches a number two higher or lower than itself, as shown in Figure 9-1.

Cutting four-way matches

1. Tape the leaves into a tight bundle in flitch order between thin plywood or MDF.
2. Cut the package on a chop saw or a table saw with a crosscut box.
3. Use the first cut edge as a reference to draw layout lines for the following cuts.

Ideas for four-way matches

Diamond and X: Cut sheets in a square shape with the grain at a 45-degree angle to the cut.

Cross and box: Cut triangular pieces with the grain at a 45-degree angle to the cut.

Figure 9-3. To preview the match, move the mirror jig around on a single leaf of veneer.

Figure 9-2. A simple mirror jig allows you to preview the veneer match. For a four-way match, slip the two mirrors into the 90-degree slots cut in the plywood plate.

Figure 9-4. To cut veneers for four-way matches, tape the leaves into a tight book and sandwich them between pieces of sacrificial plywood or MDF.

Figure 9-5. Use the chop saw or the table saw with sliding crosscut box to saw the packet of veneers. Once you have sawn one edge, use this edge as reference for making subsequent cuts.

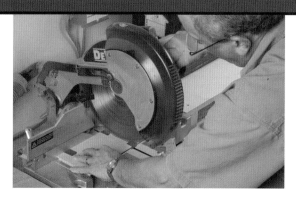

Figure 9-6. Number the cut veneers sequentially. Use white pencil on dark-colored woods.

Figure 9-7. Carefully tape the veneers together. In most four-way matches, you'll end up with two pieces face up and two face-down, as indicated by the sequential numbers.

There are several methods used to create tight seams between two leaves of veneer, as described in Chapter 2, that can be applied to a four-sheet match. However, it is very difficult to get all four pieces cut at a perfect 90-degree angle at the same time. A trick for making the four-way match go together more easily is to join them in pairs (**Figure 9-7**); then, recut the mating edges and join the two pairs.

Four-way burl match

For the top of the table detailed in this book, I will demonstrate how to create a four-way match made from burl veneer. The match will be inlaid on the surface of the tabletop. The first step is to use the mirrors to determine where to cut the veneer to create the most interesting pattern (**Figure 9-8**). Once the lines are established, rough-cut the shape a little oversize with a veneer saw, stack the four veneers together, and shoot one edge of the stack using any standard shooting jig. I generally take a sanding stick to burl veneers because it is least likely to damage their fragile edges. Then, arrange the four leaves on the benchtop to preview the match (**Figure 9-9**).

I like to join the four pieces of veneer in two steps. In this case, I will join #1 and #3 as a set and then join #2 and #4 as a second set (**Figure 9-10**). Joining the pieces can be accomplished using any standard shooting jig. After these two pairs are shot, they need to be joined to complete the pattern. You may need to recheck and, if necessary, redraw the line (**Figure 9-11**) because things may have moved around when creating the first two seams. I usually shoot both sheets at once. There are several methods that work well for accurately making a 90-degree cut when you need to either join four pieces of veneer or two pieces of veneer end to end. It is critical to be able to make an accurate 90-degree cut without chipping out the end grain of the veneer. The cut can often be accomplished using a standard veneer shooter with a sanding stick (**Figure 9-12**).

Other methods that work well for squaring the ends of veneer include the use of a table saw with a sled, a siding miter saw, or a chop saw, all with a very fine blade. The key to using any of the methods is to sandwich the veneers tightly between two sacrificial plates of wood. I often nail the whole sandwich together with finish nails placed in the waste area of the veneer and away from the cut line, as shown in **Figure 9-13**.

Figure 9-8. Use the mirror jig to decide where to cut the burl veneers. Draw the cut line on the veneers following the edge of the mirrors.

Figure 9-9. Rough-cut the burl veneers and arrange them on the workbench to preview the match.

Figure 9-10. Tape the veneers together in pairs, on the newly shot edge.

Figure 9-11. Use a straight edge to saw the two sets of taped-up leaves. Make sure the cut is at right angles to the taped edge.

Four-way burl match

1. Use the mirror jig to determine the layout of an interesting pattern.
2. Rough-cut the shape oversize.
3. Stack the four veneers together.
4. Shoot one edge of the stack using a standard shooting jig.
5. Arrange the leaves on the benchtop to preview the match.
6. Join the four pieces in two sets.

If necessary, small veneer nails or finish nails actually can penetrate the desired finish area of the veneer without causing much damage. Provided your saw is set up properly to cut a 90-degree angle, the advantage is you can get a quick and accurate cut every time without tearing out the veneer. The method is particularly suitable for highly figured and burl veneers.

After all four pieces have been matched and taped, the sheet is ready to be inlaid into the field veneer for our tabletop. One good way to check the seams and make sure all are tight is to hold the taped sheet up to the light (**Figure 9-14**). If light shines through the tape between the pieces of veneer, it is likely glue will come up through this gap, causing a line to appear on the surface. If that is the case, carefully remove the tape with a knife and reshoot the seam. You can dampen the tape to help get it off, but do not wet it or the surrounding veneer. If wet, the veneer is liable to curl up and change shape, making it difficult to create a decent seam.

Figure 9-12. Load the two pairs of taped leaves into the shooting jig and shoot the edge with a sanding stick, a method least likely to damage fragile burls.

Figure 9-13. To shoot burl veneers on the table saw, trap the fragile wood between two sacrificial plates, and tack the sandwich to the crosscut box.

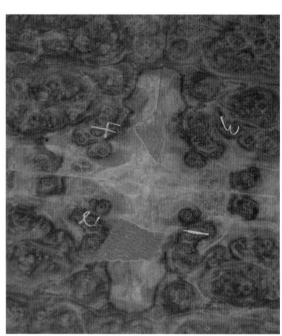

Figure 9-14. Tape the four leaves of burl together and hold them up to the light to check the match. If there are any gaps, adjust now, before proceeding to inlay the burl match.

Radial match

Beautiful radial or sunburst patterns have always been popular. The patterns have traditionally been made using veneers with a crotch, swirl, or burl, or even with veneers that have a linear straight-grain pattern (**Figure 9-15**). To create the patterns, accuracy of measuring and cutting are extremely important. If you are making a 16-piece match, any variance in the angle can be multiplied by a factor of 16, if one edge is off, or by 32 if the angle is incorrect on both sides of each piece.

To lay out the veneer pieces, first determine the proper angle to be cut. For the sunburst pattern on the dining tabletop shown in Figure 9-15, I used a 12-sheet match. If I had been a little off on one of the angles, the variance in the angle would have been multiplied by a factor of 12. If both sides were incorrect the angle would be off by a factor of 24. To determine the proper angle to cut the pieces, I divided the 360-degree circle by 12 to get 30 degrees for each section. I then divided the number in half to get 15 degrees for the angle between each leaf. For the example of the demilune tabletop detailed here, you can use the same numbers because you are making a half-circle using six pieces.

Begin by finding the place to cut the veneer using the mirror jig (**Figure 9-16**). Next, stack the pieces to be cut as close to the way they originally grew as possible and lay out the cut lines on the top piece, using the mirror jig. Before doing any cutting, extend the layout lines and verify the segment angle with a protractor (**Figures 9-17** and **9-18**). It is a good idea to place a little veneer tape on what will be the top of each sheet, right at the point where the two lines intersect and the veneer comes to a point. The tape will protect the delicate points throughout the entire cutting, fitting, and gluing process. Make sure to alternate taping the top and back face of each sheet if you are making a book match because the tape will remain on the surface until after the panel has been glued up. **Figure 9-19** shows laying out the veneers for our demilune table.

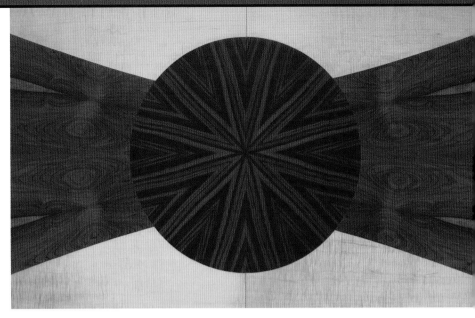

Figure 9-15. A radial match graces the center of a dining table, made by Jonathan Benson. The circle parts in the center to make space for leaves.

Figure 9-16. Lay out the radial match with the aid of the mirror jig. You can see the match in the mirrors, and draw along them to locate the saw cuts.

Figure 9-17. Extend the initial layout lines and verify the segment angle with a protractor.

Figure 9-18. A crotch mahogany radial match for a demilune table. Lay out the tabletop full size on the work surface, here a sheet of ¼" plywood.

Figure 9-19. Spread the veneers in flitch order and letter them to correspond with the lettered segments on the layout. The veneers were flattened using a glue size, and some protective newsprint remains stuck to them.

Figure 9-20. On a tricky match, it is safer to saw the veneers in pairs, mating edge to mating edge, rather than all at once.

Figure 9-21. Check the angle on each pair of veneers against the layout. Be sure each leaf is extra long.

Once all of the pieces have been carefully stacked, tape them together on two sides as shown and then rough-cut the first side of the stack to size (**Figure 9-20**). As with most rough-cutting procedures, leave ¹⁄₁₆" to ⅛" of material for the final shooting. Also, leave the pieces at least ½" long on what will be the outside of the circle (**Figure 9-21**). The extra will be trimmed after you tape the entire circle. There are two reasons for making the circle larger and trimming it later. First, the circle may end up a little uneven around the perimeter, or off round, after it's all taped. Second, each time you have to reshoot the edges to make adjustments, each segment gets a little smaller, which will result in a slightly smaller circle. The problems will disappear once you trim the circle to final size.

Next, shoot the first edges. Make sure the grain of the stack is aligned as close as possible to the way the tree originally grew. Examine the grain direction near the point of the segment, and make sure to cut the point with the grain. For veneer with grain that changes along its length, or for smaller pieces, I like to use a sanding stick as the cutter (**Figure 9-22**). A sanding stick prevents any tearout, provides more control over the cutting process by removing less material

Figure 9-22. Shoot the veneers one pair at a time. The sanding stick is safest for brittle material like this.

with each pass, and allows me to see how much material I am removing with each stroke.

After the stack has been removed from the shooter, tape the edge of the stack that was just cut, before removing the tape from the other edge. Keep tape on the end and one edge of the stack at all times to help keep the veneers from shifting. Cut and shoot the second edge of the stack.

After the second cuts have been completed, remove the pieces from the shooter and place them in a circle (**Figure 9-23**). If the angle is off, so that a little material needs to be removed from either side of the cut to make everything fit all around the circle, you will need to stack, retape, and shoot all of the sheets again. If you are making a complete circle and if you try to do one or two sheets individually, it will become almost impossible to get a perfect fit all the way around the circle. The grain will no longer match, and you may end up with an oval shape.

When all of the seams are tight, place bits of blue painter's tape on the back of the sheet as you assemble it, to get everything lined up. Tape the seams along their length on the front face of the veneer using veneer tape (**Figure 9-24**). If you have not already trimmed the butt ends of the veneers close to the layout circle, do it now. The trimming can be done with scissors for the rough-cut before taping, and with the beam compass and knife after the sheet has been taped. If you plan on adding a veneer border, make the second cut when fitting this pattern to the border veneer by cutting through both sheets at the same time (**Figure 9-25**).

Finally, remove the blue painter's tape from the back. You might end up with quite a few layers of veneer tape toward the center of the circle, but that all can be removed after the sheet has been glued down to the substrate. These techniques can be altered to create many types of interesting and stunning patterns (**Figure 9-26**).

Figure 9-23. The radial match emerges as you cut and shoot succeeding pairs of segments. When they all fit neatly together, tape the demilune with paper veneer tape on what will be the top surface.

Figure 9-24. Tape the demilune segments on the show side, and remove the blue tape from the back.

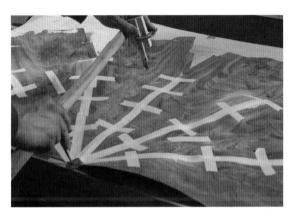

Figure 9-25. A beam compass with a sharp knife installed can trim the circular edge of this radial match.

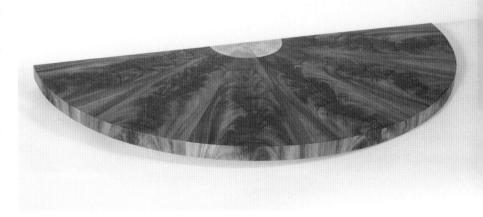

Figure 9-26. The completed, pressed, and sanded demilune top has a semicircular medallion inlaid at the center, and a veneered edge made from the segment scraps.

Understanding the Radial Match

A radial match in highly figured veneers makes a beautiful sunburst pattern, which can be used as a full circle, a semicircle, or a quarter circle. As detailed in the photo sequence on page 109, the procedure involves cutting and taping long, narrow triangles of figured veneer, and shooting the edges to a perfect seam. Twelve and sixteen points were traditionally popular, although the figure available in the veneers—as determined by studying the match using the mirror jig—will determine the best number to use. The most difficult part of achieving a perfect radial match is getting the angle of the segments exactly right. If it is off, you cannot adjust by reshooting a single point. You have to retape the entire circle or semicircle and shoot all of the veneers together. I've found a sanding stick gives me the most accurate results.

The sequence of steps is:

- Use the mirror jig to find the best match and determine the number of points in the sunburst.
- Divide 360 degrees by the number of points to get the angle of each point.
- Stack the veneers and lay out the triangular segment on the top veneer.
- Tape the stack, rough-cut the first edge, and shoot the edge.
- Tape the new edge, then rough-cut and shoot the second edge.
- Check the seams and adjust as necessary.
- Tape the sunburst, cut the segments to length, and prepare it for pressing.

Figure 9-27. Inlay one veneer into another by cutting through both using a sharp knife and a firm straightedge.

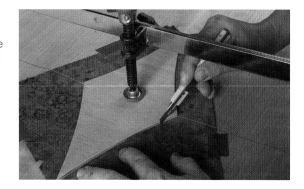

Figure 9-28. To use an inlay template, clamp it in place on the work and trace around it with the sharp knife, cutting through the inlay and the field veneer below.

Inlay

There is a fine and somewhat blurry line between inlay and marquetry, and they have many things in common. Perhaps there does not need to be a distinction between the two, but for the purposes of this book I have retained the traditional definitions. Inlay describes techniques for creating basic geometric patterns and simple curves set into a field, while marquetry describes how to make more complex pictures in wood. Both techniques involve stacking two adjoining pieces of veneer together, cutting through both of them, and then taping them side-by-side. In these veneer applications, the term inlay does not refer to routing a groove or recess in a surface into which you set a line or medallion—a much more difficult and risky process. In veneering, it refers to cutting an opening in a large field of veneer, into which to set another piece of veneer. Both the background and the piece to be inlaid can be, and usually are, taped-up assemblies of veneer. Once the inlay is completed, the entire panel can be glued onto a substrate.

For our tabletop demonstration project, we will be setting the four-way burl match into a field of veneer or making an inlay of it. We need to cut around all sides of the piece to be inlaid. To guide the knife, you can either use a straightedge or a template. I will detail both methods because each has advantages in particular situations.

The straightedge method is good for shapes with straight lines. It is fast, versatile, and accurate. Use the straightedge method for inlaying the four-way burl match, as shown in **Figure 9-27**. The template method allows the introduction of curves and irregular shapes. Templates for the knife to follow can be made of Masonite, wood, or plastic (**Figure 9-28**).

Straightedge method: layout

To begin an inlay using a straightedge and knife, draw the entire shape to be cut out on the piece of material to be inlaid. Doing so allows you to make sure all of the lines and angles are true and to see where the lines fall in relation to the figure pattern. I often make an inlay just a little bigger or smaller than I originally intended in order to capitalize on some detail within the wood figure I had not previously noticed. That is another good argument for making everything a little oversize to begin with.

Next, determine where exactly in the field the inlay will be set, and draw out the desired shape on the field. Remember, you are always cutting from the back of the sheet. Transfer lines from the inlay onto the field to make sure the inlay is set-in right where you want it, as shown in the step-by-step sequence on pages 113 and 114. I want the center of the inlay to align with the seam between the two center sheets of the background field. To quickly learn exactly where the seam is under layers of veneer tape, fold the veneer 90 degrees toward the tape side and make a line with a sharp pencil right in the corner where the two sheets join.

Attach the piece to be inlaid onto the back face of the field veneer with blue painter's tape, which can be easily removed later without damaging the veneer. Both the inlay and the field should be back side up, with the inlay on top of the back face of the veneer. Place a small piece of blue painter's tape on the inlay on any spot where the design comes to a point. The tape will discourage the little point of veneer from breaking off. Redraw the layout lines over the tape as necessary. Make some type of registration mark on the inlay and the field so after everything is cut, the inlay will go back into the field in the proper orientation (**Figure 9-29**).

I usually tape everything down to a piece of good plywood or MDF before cutting. Plywood or MDF provide a smooth, even surface to cut

on and help prevent tearout on the underside of the veneer. Being secured keeps everything from shifting and sliding during cutting and allows you to work from any angle as the entire board can be rotated and moved without shifting the veneer. Some veneer workers prefer the traditional method of taping only on the front side and tacking the veneer down with small nails. I have found it is much easier to work as described here. Tape the veneer with blue painter's tape on the back, flip the sheet over to tape the face with veneer tape. Then, remove the blue painter's tape from the back as soon as the veneer tape adhesive has dried.

Straightedge method: cutting

Both pieces are ready to be cut through at the same time. Lay the straightedge on the line and clamp it down to prevent it from slipping. I prefer to place the straightedge on the inside of the shape to be cut, so it can help hold the veneer down tight. The straightedge should remain on the inside of the cut line all the way around. If you flip it to the outside for some cuts and the inside for others, the inlay and the hole will not come out the same size. Hold the knife perpendicular to the face of the veneer at all times. Any variation in that angle will cause the inlay and the hole to be slightly different sizes, resulting in gaps. It is very important to follow the grain direction with the knife in a way that

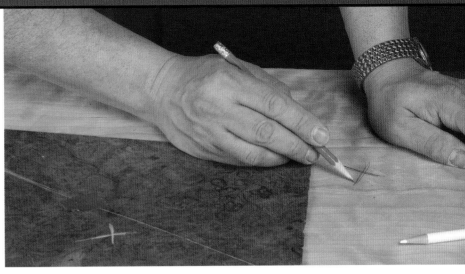

Figure 9-29. A registration mark is essential with symmetrical inlays, so you can be sure to fit the piece into the recess the right way around.

guides the knife toward the straightedge instead of away from it (**Figure 9-30**).

Make sure to use a sharp knife. I like to use a breakaway knife (Figure 9-30) with a fresh, new break-blade for each new inlay. The knives are thin enough to create a tight, gap-free seam, and thick enough to stay in the line when cutting. Utility knives are too thick, allowing gaps to appear between the two pieces. Razor blades are too thin and tend to wander away from the cut. A craft knife or a sharp scalpel also will work well for cutting out most types of inlays. They can be resharpened as needed. European-trained workers often use a wide, sharp chisel.

The first cut should not be deep at all. The main purpose of the first cut is just to create a nice valley to guide the rest of the cuts. If this first shallow cut strays from the straightedge, remember it is the underside of the sheet and if the errant cut did not penetrate deep into the veneer, it won't show later. When making each cut, it helps to stop just short of the end and finish the last bit by itself. In most cases, this will prevent the knife from traveling too far and making a longer cut than you intended.

Figure 9-30. With a thin breakaway knife like this one, keep the side of the knife tight against the straightedge, and cut with the grain of the wood.

Once the inlay has been cut out, carefully remove the waste from the edges of the inlay and the center cutout from the background field. Complete the corners as necessary while you are removing the waste. You should be able to fit the inlay precisely into the recess. Tape the inlay in place with blue painter's tape, turn the sheet over, and tape all of the seams with veneer tape on the top. Finally, remove the blue painter's tape from the back. I usually place finished veneer layups between two pieces of plywood or MDF to flatten them a little and to protect them until they are ready to be glued down.

Fitting an inlay

If the inlay does not quite fit properly, there are a few options you might try. First, it should be a very tight fit anyway, so if the inlay piece is too large, you may be able to stretch the field veneer or compress the inlay a little to force it into place. To do so, tape the inlay down on one side and apply pressure around the remaining edges with a veneer hammer. Another option is to place the inlay into a shooting jig or between two straight boards and sand a little bit off one side. Experience has shown it is difficult to fit an inlay after it has been cut out.

If these options fail, you can make either a new field veneer or a new inlay. When making a new field veneer, repeat the steps above and place the inlay on the back of the new piece of field veneer. Cut through the inlay just inside the edge all the way around the perimeter. The result will be a slightly smaller inlay, but it could save a lot of time and veneer if the inlay is complicated. If you would rather replace the inlay and retain the field veneer, make a slightly larger inlay and repeat the steps above. Level the working surface by replacing the original scrap, place the new inlay over the hole in the original field veneer, then cut around the perimeter of the inlay just outside the edge of the original hole in the field veneer.

Template method

You also can use a template made of wood, Masonite, or plastic to guide the knife for an inlay. The most difficult part of this procedure is holding down the pattern at all times without moving the clamps during the cutting process. There are several ways to accomplish it. Various types of deep reach clamps are available. There are screws that attach to existing bar clamps, such as the one shown in **Figure 9-31**. If you have a screw press, you can use one or two press screws to hold the pattern down. If there is another member passing through the inlay, you can attach the pattern with a wood screw in an area that will be covered or cut away later.

Once you have devised a method for holding the template in place on the veneer sandwich of inlay and field, the cutting methods are the same as discussed previously for straightedge and knife (**Figure 9-32**). When cutting circles and other complex shapes, it is particularly important to pay close attention to the grain direction at all times. There will be a limit to how much small detail you can cut out with a knife. If the radiuses are too tight, or if the details are too small, you can use the marquetry techniques described in the next chapter.

Pass-through inlays

You can create inlays that seem to pass through either a flat panel or a curved panel, as in the example shown in **Figure 9-33**. The key to making the illusion successful is to ensure the top and bottom panels stay properly aligned throughout the gluing process. The process can be difficult because layers of wood and veneer with glue in between tend to slide around under pressure. The solution to the problem is simple.

I have developed a two-step process that prevents almost all movement during the gluing process. The first step is to create two semi-rigid panels of thin material, which include the laid-up

Figure 9-31. The screw head attaches to the middle of a bar clamp, making it ideal for pressing an inlay template onto the work.

Figure 9-32. Use the knife to cut around an inlay template, same as the straightedge. Cut through the inlay veneer and the field veneer at the same time.

Figure 9-33. The ends of this coffee table consist of a single veneer layup bent over a form, but the dark diamond seems to be a separate piece or a pass-through piece. Perfect alignment is the key to this illusion.

face veneers. These can be created by gluing the face veneers to ⅛" MDF, to ⅛" plywood, or to a crossbanding made from ¹⁄₁₆" veneer of a similar color. The thin panel can then be screwed to the substrate before pressing the entire panel in a separate operation. For the technique to work, there must be a border of waste along the length of each face layup. Two screws placed at the

This sequence shows how to use the knife and straightedge to cut a diamond-shaped four-way burl match and inlay it into a field of cherry veneer. The example is from the demonstration tabletop that appears throughout this book, but the techniques would be the same on any project. The basic sequence is:

1. Tape the inlay onto the veneer field.
2. Use a straightedge and a breakaway knife to cut through both the inlay and field veneers.
3. Lift the cutout from the field veneer and fit the inlay into the recess.
4. Tape everything in place to prepare it for pressing.

Step 1. Use blue painter's tape to place the inlay on the taped-up field veneer. Make registration marks so you can be sure to orient the cut pieces correctly later on.

Step 2. Draw the final shape on the inlay veneers. Protect the delicate corners with extra pieces of blue painter's tape.

Step 3. Clamp a straightedge on the layout line and cut with a thin, sharp knife. The batten helps clamp the straightedge; the veneers under it put pressure right on the cut line.

Step 4. Make several passes to cut through both the inlay and the field veneer. Be sure to cut exactly to each corner, or stop just short and finish the corners while removing the waste.

Step 5. Separate the waste from the inlay, and be sure to make a witness mark (the X at upper right). Then, lift the cut inlay itself out of the way.

Step 6. Carefully remove the cutout from the field veneer. You might have to do more knife work before it separates completely.

Step 7. Fit the inlay into the recess. Be sure to align it using your registration mark. Hold it there with blue tape.

Step 8. Flip the sheet over and carefully press the inlay into the recess. It should fit exactly. Tape it there using paper veneer tape.

Step 9. Be sure to tape the joints in the inlay itself, too. With the inlay taped in, the layup is ready to be pressed onto a substrate.

center of this border will prevent the layers from shifting. The screws are removed after the glue has dried and before the panel is trimmed.

To make the technique work best, use only two screws at the center of each border on each face of the panel. Doing so allows the sheets to lie flat as pressure is applied. If there were screws along the entire border, the layers would be trapped between the screws and would be prevented from flattening out, causing ripples and gaps. The technique described works for curved panels as well.

Routing inlays

Using a router, inlays can be set into a flat surface that already has been glued together. There are two-part jigs available that will create the same shape when cutting the hole and the piece to be inlaid. The router jigs work with guide collars

that compensate for the radius of the cutter. The piece to be inlaid is usually backed with a crossband veneer, to strengthen the inlay and prevent it from breaking apart.

Attach the inlay piece to a scrap piece of wood with temporary adhesive or double-stick tape. The template, which consists of a board or piece of plastic with a hole in the shape of the desired inlay, is clamped securely over the inlay and the scrap board. The exact size to make the hole in the template is determined by the router bit and the instructions for the particular router jig you choose. The inlay is then cut out and the template is removed. After determining the proper depth to cut with scrap wood and the actual piece to be inlaid, the template is transferred onto the background surface. Finally the hole for the inlay is cut, and if the router guide collars were correctly chosen, the inlay should fit exactly into the hole. This process works best with designs with curved corners, ovals, and circles, though right-angled corners can be achieved with a little foresight and a sharp chisel.

Borders

Many veneered projects have some type of border around the design. A border can add much visual interest, plus it will help to define and emphasize the design itself. Strips to create a border can be made using the parquetry techniques described above. Many types of commercially available border material, often referred to as banding, can be purchased as well. These can add a lot of interest to a design without a lot of work. Some of the more intricate patterns would be extremely difficult to create with small pieces of veneer. You do need to have border material in hand before beginning a project to make sure its thickness is close to that of the veneer with which you plan to combine it.

I usually make simple borders and apply them to the veneer sheet before it is glued down. Borders are often created using veneer with strong linear qualities, such as Macassar ebony or zebrawood. The veneer can be cut lengthwise into strips, or crosswise to the grain and laid side by side.

There are several methods for applying borders. I prefer to tape the border material to the rest of the veneer before attaching the entire sheet to the substrate, as shown the step-by-step sequence. Taping will work best if the substrate panel remains a little oversize until the gluing process is completed allowing room for the veneer to shift on the wet glue surface as you apply pressure. You can trim the panel right to the outside edge of the border after the glue has set.

Inlaid border

If you have a panel with an edge that needed to be applied prior to attaching the veneer, or if the border or banding is significantly thicker than the rest of the veneer, the border can be inlaid into the substrate after applying the laid-up veneer. This is done in several steps.

First, the field veneer needs to be cut through with a sharp knife to prevent tearout. Guide the knife with a straightedge or template that is securely fastened down. As with the inlay process described above, try to follow the grain so it guides the knife toward the straightedge or template. Start with a very shallow cut for the knife to ride.

Create an Inlaid Border

To recap, the sequence for an inlaid border is:
1. Anticipate and prevent tearout by knife-cutting through the field veneers, using a clamped straightedge or a template.
2. Template-rout, or use the same straightedge as a guide, to cut a recess for the inlay or border.
3. Fit the border or inlay in place, tape it to the face veneer, and clamp it.

Once you believe you have cut through the face veneer, the rest of the veneer can be removed with a router, using a following bit with the bearing on top guided by that same template. If the router has a straight cutting bit (I recommend a spiral-cutting mill bit with four cutters), you can use a fence to guide the router base. Test the depth to make sure the border and the rest of the panel end up level and even—veneer leaves little room for leveling by sanding.

The border veneer can then be glued down. Lay the border veneer down next to the field veneer and veneer-tape the entire length. Then, fold the border veneer back over on the tape like a hinge, and apply glue to the substrate only, but make sure to get a little glue along the edge of the inner veneer, too. Fold the veneer down and apply pressure with clamps and cauls.

Rolled edge border

Veneer can be rolled over the edge of a panel using a vacuum bag for pressure. An MDF substrate is first routed or shaped to its final contour. The veneer has to be applied in two steps.

First, apply an oversize veneer layup to the flat surface of the top. The veneer has to be large enough to roll over the edge later, though in this first step, you'll only glue it to the flat portion of the panel. Place blue painter's tape over the curved edge to prevent glue from getting on this surface. Spread PVA glue such as Titebond or Titebond II on the flat surface of the panel only, being careful not to get any on the rounded edge.

Place the veneer over the top and put it in the vacuum bag with a flat caul large enough to cover the veneer. Because the caul is oversize, you may need to place a strip of wood under the overhang to support the caul and prevent it from breaking off under the pressure. Place everything in the vacuum bag and leave it under pressure for one hour.

When you take the panel out of the vacuum bag, remove the blue tape and apply glue to the

This sequence shows how to add a border of contrasting veneer to a taped-up tabletop veneer. The example is one of the veneered tabletops prepared for the demonstration sequence that runs throughout this book. The walnut border has mitered corners, and is knife-cut with a straightedge–the method I find most flexible and reliable.

The basic sequence is:

1. Tape the border veneers onto the veneer field. Overlap the corners for a miter.
2. Use a straightedge and a breakaway knife to cut through both the border and field veneers.
3. Flip the layup over to tape the face with paper tape. Remove the blue tape from the back side.
4. Press the layup onto a substrate and trim to final size afterward.

Step 1. Working on the back side of the layup and from the center of the book-match, carefully lay out the edges of the panel. Check that the layout is square by measuring the diagonals.

Step 2. Use scissors to cut oversize strips of border veneer, in this case walnut to set against the cherry field.

Step 3. Use blue painter's tape to attach the border veneers to the field, and transfer the layout lines onto the top surface.

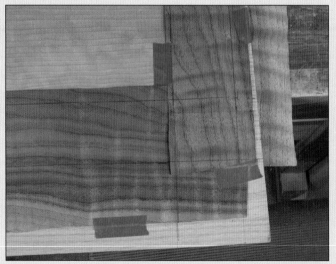

Step 4. Overlap the border veneers at the corner so you can make a miter by cutting through both layers at once.

Step 5. Clamp a metal straightedge on the layout line and cut through the border veneer and the field veneer at the same time.

Step 6. Flip the sheet over to carefully remove all of the cut-through scraps.

Step 7. Working on the face of the layup, apply paper veneer tape to the joint between the border and the field veneers.

Step 8. Finally, turn the layup over again and remove all of the blue tape. Now it is ready to be glued to a substrate. Trim it to final size after gluing up.

Rolled edge border

1. Route an MDF substrate to its final contour.
2. Apply an oversize veneer layup to the flat surface of the top. The veneer has to be large enough to roll over the edge later.
3. Put blue painter's tape over the curved edge to keep glue from oozing out.
4. Spread PVA glue on the flat surface of the panel only. Do not get any on the rounded edge.
5. Put the veneer over the top with a flat caul large enough to cover the veneer.
6. Place a strip of wood under the overhang to support the caul and keep it from breaking under the pressure.
7. Put the setup in the vacuum bag and leave it under pressure for an hour.
8. Take the panel out of the bag and remove the blue tape.
9. Apply glue to the edge under the veneer.
10. Put the arrangement back in the vacuum bag without a caul and begin to apply pressure. The veneer should form over the edge and seal down tightly. Help with a small rubber roller if necessary. In Chapter 7, I demonstrated making a solid wood edging with an inlaid band around it for the demonstration tabletop. Most of the photo sequences in Chapter 9 revolve around making the tabletop inlay and applying a veneer border to the panel. Here's a recap of the process:

Shop-made banding for borders

1. Stack and glue several layers of contrasting veneer.
2. Cut the sandwich into strips of the desired angle and size.
3. Lay the strips side-by-side and glue them between more sheets of veneer.
4. Slice strips of border material off the glued-up block.
5. Lay the strips end-to-end to create the border.

edge under the veneer. Next, put the top back into the vacuum bag without any cauls. Begin to apply pressure and the veneer should form over the edge and seal down tight. You can help it with a small rubber roller.

The same method also will work for chamfered edges if you apply tape to the areas that will have to bend, which keeps the veneer from tearing apart. I have also seen the same method used on a round tabletop with a bull-nosed edge. It takes a little practice to get the veneer to conform to the curve, and it helps to have a vacuum pump that can be regulated with a foot pedal to control how fast and when the air is removed. You can also combine this method with the technique of hammer veneering (page 71) to veneer over a curved edge.

Shop-made banding

You can create your own banding in several steps. First, stack several layers of contrasting veneer or thinly cut wood and glue them into a sandwich. Cut the sandwich into strips of the desired angle and size. Lay the strips side-by-side and glue them between more sheets of veneer to create another sandwich. Strips of border material can be sliced like lunch meat off the glued-up block. The pieces are then laid end-to-end to create the border. You might find you cannot saw the strips as thin as the veneer they are to border. Consequently, you won't be able to tape this type of banding to the rest of the veneer before gluing it down. You'll have to inlay it around the veneer field after the main glue-up.

In Chapter 7, I demonstrated making a solid wood edging with an inlaid band around it for the demonstration tabletop. Most of the photo sequences in Chapter 9 revolve around making the tabletop inlay and applying a veneer border to the panel. Here's a recap of the process.

Step 1. Saw, joint, and tape up the four bookmatched leaves that comprise the field veneer. Use blue tape on the back side, and paper veneer tape on the show side.

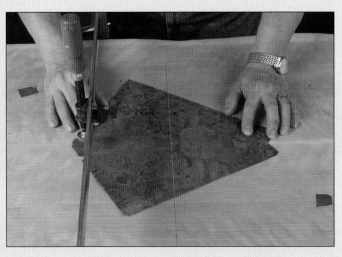

Step 2. Match and join the burl inlay veneers, and center them on the field veneers.

Step 3. With an inlay template or a straightedge, cut through both the inlay veneers and the field veneers using a sharp knife.

Step 4. Tape the inlay into the field veneers, add a border veneer, and remove the blue tape from the back side. The panel is ready to press.

CHAPTER 10

Marquetry & Parquetry

To create intricate, detailed, and beautiful pictures in wood, pictorial marquetry and geometric parquetry techniques can be employed. Making pictures from small, thin pieces of wood and joining them together as surface decoration has a long history in both Western and Eastern art. Some of the earliest examples combine wood with gems, precious metals, and other materials. For the woodworker, it is a great way to use up small pieces of veneer that are too beautiful to throw away. Many veneer suppliers sell end-cuts, shorts, and mismatched veneer at greatly reduced prices and they make perfect material for many marquetry projects.

Marquetry encompasses many techniques incorporating various saws and knives. Handsaws with a thin blade, such as a fret saw, and powered scroll saws are well-suited for cutting intricate curves in thin material, including veneer. Other materials, such as mother-of-pearl, metal, and plastic can be combined with wood to create interesting and unusual designs.

I will begin with a discussion of the sawing techniques used in marquetry and then show how to combine them with the knife-cutting techniques. You will see how each has its own advantages and disadvantages and how you might want to combine them in a particular project.

Elaborate pictorial illusions are common in traditional marquetry, and contemporary artist Silas Kopf has carried on the tradition with *Cats and Books*, a fall-front desk. The cat, the cabinet doors, and the drawer are all marquetry representations.

Marquetry sawing techniques

There are two types of handsaw that can be used for marquetry. The type of saw that has been used for centuries in one form or another is the fretsaw. It is like a coping saw (**Figure 10-1**), except it has an extra-deep throat for reaching into the middle of large designs. The fret saw can be expensive and hard to find. Jewelry saws work very well for marquetry. They are relatively inexpensive, are available in various sizes, and will hold a variety of different size blades. The extremely thin blades can easily cut around the most intricate designs, and they also can be threaded through a tiny hole to cut an interior shape. The hole could be drilled, but if you make it with a sewing needle, it will all but disappear when you finish the piece. A standard coping saw does not work too well for marquetry because it is difficult to find blades thin enough.

To make two adjoining pieces of veneer the same shape, it is easiest to place one piece on top of the other and cut them at the same time. However, if you were to make a 90-degree cut through both pieces, there would be a gap the thickness of the saw blade. The gap is the same as the saw kerf that results from any saw cut. To compensate for the kerf and create a tight fit all around the shape, the saw can be tilted a few degrees. This will create a wedge-shaped inlay slightly larger than the hole into which it fits (**Figure 10-2**). The technique is called double-bevel sawing.

The exact angle of the saw cut depends on the thickness of the blade and the thickness of the

Figure 10-1. You can get started in marquetry using a standard coping saw, though you will be able fit finer blades into a jeweler's saw.

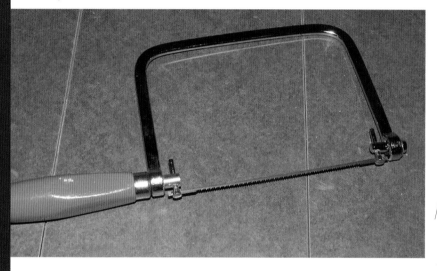

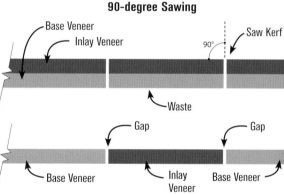

90-degree Sawing

Base Veneer
Inlay Veneer
90°
Saw Kerf
Waste
Gap
Gap
Base Veneer
Inlay Veneer
Base Veneer

Double-bevel Sawing

Base Veneer
Inlay Veneer
Angle depends on kerf and veneer thickness.
Saw Kerf
Waste
No Gap
Base Veneer
Inlay Veneer
Base Veneer

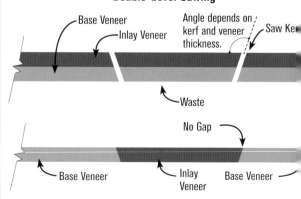

Figure 10-2. In double-bevel sawing, the saw is held at an angle so the veneer piece will drop neatly into the space cut out for it, eliminating the gap caused by the saw kerf.

Marquetry TERMS

Coping saw. A U-shaped saw frame with a wooden handle, which takes standard pin-end blades, is a coping saw. Can be used to saw veneers and thin wood in intricate shapes.

Double-bevel sawing. A shape sawn from two layers of veneer with the saw held at an angle of about 15 degrees, so the top piece will drop into the cutout in the bottom piece with no gaps, is called double-bevel sawing.

Jeweler's saw. An adjustable saw frame with a pin vise at each end that can accept extremely fine blades is a jeweler's saw. Can make a finer cut than a coping saw.

Sand shading. Shading light-colored veneers by scorching them in hot sand is called sand shading. This technique is used for marquetry pictures.

Sawing table. A small work platform mounted on a raised stake, on which marquetry pieces can be sawn, is a sawing table. It's also called a bird's mouth because of the deep V usually cut into the table.

Figure 10-3. A simple bird's-mouth sawing table, held in the bench vise, is all you need to begin sawing marquetry.

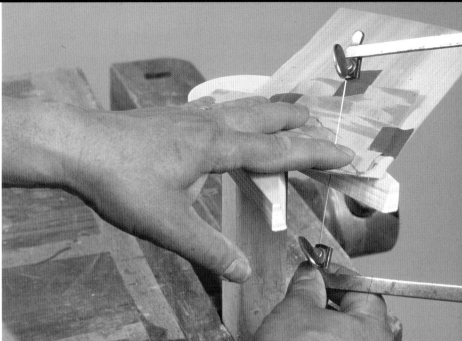

Figure 10-4. The veneers to be sawn rest on the sawing table, while the coping saw, fretsaw, or jeweler's saw works in the space between the two arms.

veneer. You will need to experiment with some scrap veneer to determine the exact angle that works best. I have found that with most veneers sold today, and using a fine #00 blade, the angle of tilt is 12 to 15 degrees. When hand-sawing you have to hold the saw at the proper angle. I like to cut a block of wood to the bevel angle and keep it nearby as a visual aid.

When using the double-bevel sawing technique, the top surface you see usually will be taped with veneer tape and thus will become the outside surface of the finished panel. The two adjoining pieces to be cut are placed in a sandwich, with a backer veneer on the bottom. The backer veneer, which should have its grain running in the opposite direction to the finish layers, will prevent tearout under the bottom layer.

When sawing by hand you will need to support the veneer from the underside while it is being cut. A shop-made table similar to the one shown in **Figure 10-3** will support the veneer at a point very close to where the cut actually is being made. The table can be tilted to the bevel angle and rotated as needed. Using a table, the handsaw

Figure 10-5. A scroll saw works well for marquetry. Tilt the table to the double-bevel angle, and rotate the sandwich of veneers as you make the cut.

is easy to control and beginners can see good results quickly (**Figure 10-4**).

Scroll saws also will work very well for marquetry (**Figure 10-5**). They can be a little tricky at first—they move fast and are a little harder to control—but with a little practice, they can all but replace handsaws for most designs. For best results, use the thinnest possible blade.

Marquetry Patterns

To start with marquetry, choose a relatively simple design with two or three types of veneer, and then work up to more complicated designs. Start by drawing a pattern (**Figure 10-6**) or purchasing one where woodworking supplies are sold. I usually transfer the pattern to tracing paper so I can see the details of the wood figure through the paper. Also, you might want to make more than one copy because, as the cutting progresses and more species of veneers are added, the paper will break down. I usually make several photocopies of the original pattern. If the design is too large to be photocopied, make

copies of the most detailed sections so you will have a copy for each species of wood. When creating a design larger than the depth of your saw, you will need to start in the center and build out to the border, or make the design in sections and assemble them later.

Begin by attaching the drawing to the background field veneer into which you will set the marquetry picture. There are several methods for attaching the drawing to the surface of the veneer and for bonding the sandwich together so the pieces do not slip during cutting. The requirements are that everything will need to be easily separated, without destroying the veneer and without leaving adhesive residue on the surface (residue will repel glue on the underside and finish on the surface). I often will combine attachment methods to suit the design. Some of these attachment methods are listed below.

Rubber cement. Rubber cement can be applied on one of the two surfaces to be bonded. It allows the layers to be separated after cutting and is relatively easy to clean off the surface.

Blue painter's tape. Blue tape can be placed around the edges and on the underside of the veneer where needed. Tape would allow small inlaid pieces to slip around toward the end of each cut, but you can avoid that by adding new tape as the cut progresses.

Double-stick tape. Thin double-stick tape that is designed to be easily removed works well for stacking veneer. If the tape is too sticky, attach a length of it to your clothing or a rag first. This will remove a little adhesive from the tape and add some lint to the surface, decreasing the adhesion just enough to make the tape easily removable.

Spray adhesive. Choose a spray adhesive designed to create a temporary bond. Never spray the adhesive directly on the veneer; instead, spray it onto the back of the pattern and allow it to dry for a few minutes before placing the pattern on the veneer. To stack layers of veneer, spray

Figure 10-6. A marquetry pattern can be a simple pencil drawing, right. The drawing was used to generate the taped-up picture in the center, and the finished panel at bottom.

adhesive on the top surface of the paper, allow it to dry, and place the next layer of veneer over it. You will need to experiment to see how much adhesive to use because each brand of adhesive will bond differently.

Attach the portion of the pattern that coincides with each type of wood to that wood and place it on the field veneer. If the veneer fails or something goes wrong, you can make that portion again, just slightly larger, as long as you are cutting new veneer at all times.

Sawing marquetry

Before cutting, you may need to drill a least one, or possibly more, starter holes for the saw blade. That will be the case if the field in the design totally surrounds the design to be inlaid. The drill holes can be worked into the design and filled, or the design can be altered to minimize the starter holes. I try to plan for any drill holes to end up in a dark area, making them easy to hide. You also may be able to begin a cut in an area that will be removed later, for example, by cutting through the part of the flower that will later become the stem in the step-by-step example shown later in this chapter.

As you begin to cut, you will need to hold the saw at the bevel angle in the proper orientation with the piece, to make sure the inner piece remains a true wedge shape. Always experiment with samples of the veneer to determine the bevel angle that leaves no gaps between the pieces. When cutting with a scroll saw, if the table is tilted down on the left, you will need to rotate the workpiece in a counterclockwise direction with the inlay piece downhill from the blade. With a handsaw, you likely will be cutting in the opposite direction along a given line, with the saw traveling counterclockwise and the workpiece rotating clockwise.

Once each final piece has been cut, tape it either with blue painter's tape on the underside, or preferably with veneer tape on the top, before

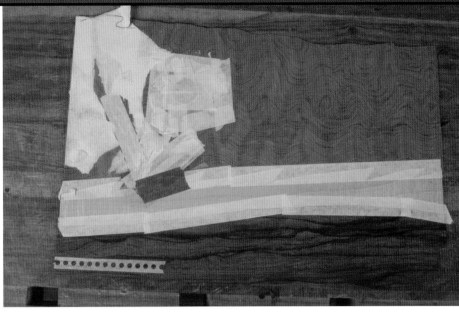

Figure 10-7. The top of the marquetry picture soon becomes covered with paper veneer tape holding the various pieces in place, and remnants of the paper pattern used to guide the sawing.

proceeding to the next cut. There may be many layers of tape on the surface before you complete the project (**Figure 10-7**).

When pressing the sheet down during the gluing process, I will sometimes place several layers of clean newsprint between the surface and the caul to relieve some of the pressure and greatly reduce the possibility of the tape indenting the surface. After removing any marquetry panel from the press or clamps, let the glue cure for a day or two. Curing will greatly reduce the chance of any grain being pulled out when you remove the tape. Allow it to dry where air can get to both sides to prevent cupping or bowing.

Basic marquetry project

If you are teaching yourself veneering and marquetry, it will be best to begin with a simple project and work up to more complicated designs later. The floral design provided here (Figure 10-6) combines several basic sawing and knife-cutting techniques. The saw cuts were executed using a 16" scroll saw with a #00 blade. You might need to alter the design a little to accommodate a handsaw, depending on the depth of the saw's throat, but otherwise the procedures should remain basically the same. The knife cuts were done with a sharp breakaway blade. Marquetry

Figure 10-8. Here is the simple flower design in marquetry, after sanding and finishing with sprayed lacquer.

sawing is done from the top side of the veneer, while knife-cutting is done from the back side, in both cases to minimize gaps caused by the cutting tool.

If you are planning on creating your own design the first time out, here are a few pointers. A somewhat abstracted organic shape allows you to incorporate mistakes into the design. Trying to replicate something exactly is an important part of marquetry and should be an attainable goal after you familiarize yourself with the basic techniques. Avoid too many sharp curves and small details in your first project. And stick with just a few species of woods to reduce the complexity.

The flower design, shown completed in **Figure 10-8**, is 16" x 11" in size. Any cut on the surface can be accomplished using a 16-inch scroll saw without hitting the machine's back riser. I like to make several copies of the drawing to use as the work progresses. In any design, always start at the center and work out to the edges. That approach allows for the construction of large designs and minimizes the number of drill holes that will have to be filled later.

Prepare the Field

I attached a copy of the drawing to the center of the dark-colored background or field veneer using the spray adhesive method. This makes the drawing resemble a giant piece of masking tape

that won't slide around and helps to keep the wood fibers together during cutting. The drawing will stay in place throughout most of the cutting. If the spray adhesive is formulated for temporary use and you apply it only to the paper and allow it to dry sufficiently before applying the paper to the veneer, it will be easy to remove the paper later without leaving any adhesive residue on the veneer.

Place a piece of veneer with the grain running in the opposite direction under the field veneer to act as a backer, which will help prevent the field from tearing out during the cutting process. The backer veneer can be attached with spray adhesive, or just taped around the edges. When the field veneer is very brittle, I glue another piece of paper to the back of the veneer to help secure the grain a little more.

Sawing the Veneers

You are ready to proceed with the first cut. For the flower design, the saw can enter through the center of what will become the stem, allowing you to start most of the cuts without remounting the blade each time. Use the double-bevel cutting method, with the scroll saw table tilted down on the left, as shown in Figure 10-5. The petal should remain on the downhill side of the blade at all times. Turn the field veneer in a counter-clockwise direction during the cut, to maintain the orientation of the bevel.

After cutting the petal, turn off the saw and back the blade out through the stem. Remove the scrap material that was outside of the petal veneer from the face of the field veneer. Be careful to leave the original drawing attached to the field veneer in the areas that have not yet been cut. If the original drawing does get damaged, adhere a new copy over the original where needed.

Tape the Petal in Place

The inlay piece should now be a sandwich of three petal shapes. Separate them and discard the backer layer piece. Replace the scrap that was originally from the field veneer into the hole in the backer veneer and tape it with blue painter's tape. Set the petal inlay in place and secure it with veneer tape on the top surface. That will allow you to overlap the next petal without tearing out the back of the first one. Complete the flower and leaves in the same manner.

Sand Shading

You can add variation to simple marquetry shapes by shading them in hot sand before taping them in place. **Figure 10-9** shows the set-up: an old frying pan on an electric hot plate. Use fine white sand, and set the hot plate for maximum. Leave the pieces in the sand for a few minutes, but make several test pieces as well so you can monitor progress.

Knife-Cut the Grass

For the flower design the grass area was inlaid using the knife technique. Up to this point, all of the work was done with what will be the top surface of the veneer up and exposed. All knife-cutting procedures are done on the backside of the veneer. The design can be transferred to the back of the veneer using transparent tracing paper. Place the light-colored wood under the field and secure it with tape. Use a sharp knife to cut through both layers, as discussed in Chapter 9. A straightedge can be used to guide the knife, but in this case, there is a slight curve to each line, so it was cut freehand. If you cut freehand, make sure to make an accurate shallow cut first, which will guide the knife for the rest of the cutting process.

Complete the Marquetry

The darker contrasting earth area can be fitted using either a saw or knife, depending on the veneer used and the complexity of the design.

Figure 10-9. Small elements such as flower petals can be given depth by sand shading.

Hard, brittle veneer may be easier to cut with a saw, and small details may be difficult to cut with a knife. The darker leaves at the very bottom of the base were applied last to finish the flower. Finally, the clouds can be bevel-cut using the saw or cut with a knife. The entire sheet can now be glued to either a flat or curved substrate.

The Marquetry Sequence

Marquetry looks complicated and there certainly can be a lot of tape holding veneers in place, but it is a logical process that generally follows the same sequence of steps:

- Simplify the proposed design as much as possible, and make multiple copies.
- Use spray adhesive to fasten the drawing onto the field veneer, and support the wood fibers with a piece of cross-grain veneer adhered to the back.
- Adhere copies of the pattern onto each different veneer to be used in the picture.
- Tape one of the picture veneers into position on the field veneer and use the double-bevel method to saw through the backer, field veneer, and picture veneer.
- Remove the waste and tape the cut piece of field veneer into the backer veneer, to make a solid ground for the picture veneer.
- Fit and tape the picture veneer into the recess in the field veneer. If the sawing bevel was correct, it will precisely fill the space.
- Repeat for all of the elements in the picture. Some of them may be simple enough to knife-cut from the back of the sheet rather than sawn from the top.
- As with simpler inlays, apply paper veneer tape to the top surface, and then remove the backer veneer and any pattern pieces and blue painter's tape from the bottom surface.
- The marquetry picture is ready to be glued onto a substrate.

Parquetry

Another way to create stunning visual effects with veneer is the technique known as parquetry (**Figure 10-11**). Parquetry, which can be defined as geometric patterns in wood, has been popular throughout history. It became particularly advanced in the Renaissance, in eighteenth-century Europe, and in the Art Deco style of the twentieth century. Its roots in technique go back to ancient Egypt. In design terms, the roots of Western parquetry can be traced back to the influence of early Islamic art, which avoided many realistic depictions and forbade human imagery. The result was a rise in spectacular geometric and floral designs in a variety of materials, including wood.

Many types of unusual geometric patterns can be created by combining contrasting woods or by combining woods of the same species with different figure orientations. Patterns can be a simple checkerboard (**Figure 10-12**) or a very complex mosaic. Some patterns appear to be three-dimensional. You can also create interesting parquetry patterns using a single species of wood, either by alternating the orientation of the grain on adjoining pieces or by capitalizing on the refractive qualities of the wood. The latter is particularly effective when creating the herringbone pattern shown in **Figure 10-13**.

To do it, select a wood that has good satin-like qualities or one that appears much lighter or darker depending on which side you view it from. Lay the two sheets side-by-side, walk around them in a circle, and observe how they seem to become lighter and darker as you move. As you move halfway around them, the sheet that was at first light should become the dark one, and vice versa. If that is indeed the case, you have made a good choice for a parquetry project. Follow the steps below to create a contrasting pattern. Labeling the top and bottom of each piece as it is being cut will help to avoid much confusion as the project progresses.

As with marquetry, I recommend starting in parquetry with a simple design first, then progressing to more complex designs. The chessboard shown in Figure 10-12 is a good place to start and begins by selecting two contrasting veneers. The step-by-step sequence will produce a checkerboard that is 16" square, for which you can create a border as discussed in Chapter 9.

Figure 10-12. A parquetry chessboard is quite simple to make from two veneers of contrasting color.

Figure 10-13. Light refraction makes the dark veneers appear to be two different colors, giving this herringbone parquetry pattern a three-dimensional effect.

A parquetry chessboard is an ingenious example of the technique. It's made by sawing and taping strips of contrasting veneers side by side then crosscutting them into strips that consist of alternating squares. These strips may then be recombined to create the checkerboard pattern. This same approach can be used to create many other geometric effects.

Step 1. Saw strips of contrasting veneers slightly oversize, 2¼" wide x 21" long. The project uses curly maple for the white squares and fiddleback makoré for the dark squares. Saw five of one color and four of the other.

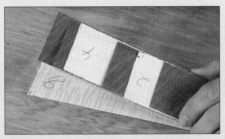

Step 2. Stack the strips in sequential order with alternating colors and with alternating faces of each species facing up for a book-matched effect, or with the same face up for a slip-matched effect. Number each sheet, and then tape the stack on both ends and one long side.

Step 3. Place the stack in the veneer shooter and shoot the first edge. Remove the top and bottom strip from the stack. They will be on the outer edges of the finished design, and you will want to trim them along with the substrate after glue-up.

Step 4. Restack the remaining sheets and tape them together, aligning the just completed edges. Tape the stack on both ends and on the shot edge. Measure over 2" from the trimmed side. Place the stack back into the shooter to prepare the unshot edge.

Step 5. After shooting the second edge, you will have seven interior strips exactly 2" wide and 21" long and two slightly wider outer strips. Lay them out side-by-side in their original order and veneer-tape them together.

Step 6. Draw lines 2¼" apart across the strips, and number each new strip. Cut down the center of each line with a veneer saw or a knife and a straightedge. Add blue tape on the back as needed to keep the strips together.

Step 7. Stack the strips in order, tape the ends, and shoot the first edge. Remove the stack, set aside the two edge strips, and retape the stack. Draw marks 2" over from the first cut on the top sheet and shoot the final edge.

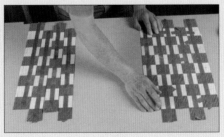

Step 8. Slide alternating strips so the chessboard pattern appears, and then tack them together with blue tape. You'll have extra squares along the edge—these will be cut off later.

Step 9. Flip the taped chessboard and apply paper veneer tape to the top surface. Remove the blue tape from the back, and the panel is ready for trimming and pressing.

CHAPTER 11

Band-Sawing Veneers

Using the band saw and other common woodworking machines, it is possible for a craftsman to reap all of the advantages of veneer by using existing solid lumber.

Veneer was sawn by hand and later by using circular saws and band saws until the introduction of the mechanical veneer slicer. The slicer allowed veneer to be cut much thinner, more quickly than by sawing, and without the waste that resulted from the thickness of the saw blade. This technology made veneering more economical and accessible, but it also removed the craftsman from the process of getting his own veneer from the plank or log.

The advantages of being able to produce your own veneer include being able to place a thin slice of the lumber inside a frame, book-match it, bend it, or use it in outdoor applications where thicker veneer is desirable.

Veneer can be band sawn from thick planks and small logs.

Why band saw?

Thin pieces of wood will bend. If several layers of thin wood are glued together and clamped onto a curved form, the resulting bent lamination will be stronger than solid wood. If the layers are kept in sequential order throughout the entire cutting and bending process, it can be very difficult to distinguish the lamination from solid wood.

In addition, some applications might require a thicker veneer of a certain species not available commercially. Only a few types of types of veneer are commercially available in ¹⁄₁₆" thickness, such as red oak, white oak, ash, mahogany, maple, and sometimes a few others. These thick veneers usually are not available with unusual types of figure, such as curl, swirl, or burl.

Finally, a unique log or thick board will go farther, covering four to five times as much surface area, by converting it to veneer instead of sawing it into boards. The procedure for sawing your own veneer is simple, provided your machines are sharp, in tune, and used carefully.

Sawing basics

Veneer should be sawn and planed to end up no thicker than ⅛" (¹⁄₁₆" is better). Otherwise, it may continue to move due to seasonal changes. If veneer is cut too thick, the bottom surface attached to the substrate will stay in place, while the top surface of the veneer will still be able to move. This will cause cracks to appear on the surface of the veneer. Wood movement also can cause the veneer to separate from the substrate. I have heard of a case where veneer that was not cut thinly enough popped off the surface of a table during a gallery opening featuring the work. That makes a strong case for getting the veneer thin enough and gluing it down properly.

Making sure machinery is properly tuned and has sharp blades and knives will get the maximum yield from the log or board. In addition, the sawn veneer needs to be properly handled and stored to prevent loss.

The material to be cut must be dry and ready to use. You can saw green lumber and logs into veneers, but the drying process becomes much more complicated. The basic sequence is to joint one surface and edge flat, smooth, and square to another. Run the face against the band saw fence. Repeat the process of jointing and sawing until all veneers have been cut. After cutting, they can be planed to final thickness. They could instead be thickness-sanded in a wide-belt machine, removing the band saw marks from their back sides in the process.

The Band Saw

The band saw used for the project must have enough throat depth between the table and the upper guide to accommodate the thickness of the wood. This dimension will become the width of the veneer after it has been cut. The saw should also have enough power to avoid slowing down or stopping when making a deep cut. Slowing down during the cutting process will dull the blade, cause burns on the surface of the wood, and make it difficult to maintain a straight cut. A resawing type of band saw works well for this operation, as does a good 20" or larger band saw, although it is possible to get good results from the common 14" saw with a riser block added to give the machine a 12" throat depth.

I like to use a new blade when beginning any band saw veneer project. A ¾"- to 1"-wide blade with four to six teeth per inch (TPI) will work quickly. Because it is wide, it will be relatively easy to keep cutting in a straight line. The saw should have a good set of roller bearings and guide blocks properly aligned. Finally, the table needs to be exactly 90 degrees to the blade. Any variance in the angle will decrease the yield of veneer by removing more material than is necessary. For details on tuning up your band saw, consult a good handbook devoted to the subject. The proper use of the ripping fence will be covered later in this chapter.

The Planer

A properly tuned planer with sharp knives is essential for producing good-quality band-sawn veneer without a lot of waste. Sharp knives keep thin pieces of veneer from tearing out or breaking apart. Having the feed and pressure rollers cleaned and properly tensioned keeps the veneer moving through the planer at a consistent speed without stopping and starting, avoiding burn marks, ridges, and valleys on its surface.

The planer's knives need to be as sharp as possible to increase the yield of veneer by reducing tearout, splitting, and even total disintegration of some sheets. The grain orientation, page 139, also has a tremendous impact on the quality of the cut. The machine's bed rollers may or may not be an issue, depending on the backing board you choose.

Increasing the planer's cutting speed will produce a smoother surface. The faster the cutting speed, the less material each knife must remove every time it contacts the wood. Planers with a speed adjustment for the cutter head should be set to the highest rpm. Using a cutter head with four knives will make a smoother cut than a cutter head with only two knives by, in effect, doubling the cutting speed. The cutting speed also can be increased by slowing down the feed rate of the wood through the planer—many machines have this adjustment.

The Jointer

Like the planer, the jointer needs to be properly tuned, with sharp knives. The outfeed table and the knives need to be properly aligned so a uniform amount of material is removed from the wood at both the beginning and the end of each pass. As with the planer, a cutter head with four knives will make a smoother cut than a cutter head with just two knives. A higher rpm setting also will create a smoother cut.

When using a jointer, the operator controls the feed rate. The feed rate can be slowed down to a point just before burn marks begin to appear, creating a surface on the wood that is as smooth as glass. The grain orientation also will have an impact on the quality of the cut. The jointer will need a sturdy fence, exactly 90 degrees to the cutter, to further maximize the yield. When cutting many pieces of veneer, it is beneficial to recheck the fence occasionally to be certain it has remained square.

Preparing the wood

Before sawing veneers from a thick piece of wood, it is necessary to create two smooth perpendicular surfaces. Start by smoothing one face of the board on the jointer (**Figure 11-1**). The figure pattern of this face will become the figure pattern for all the subsequent sheets of veneer cut from the board. If working from a log or an irregular shaped piece of wood, you may need to balance the desirability of the figure pattern with the yield that results from that particular shape. To see what types of grain patterns might be expected from cutting the wood at various angles, please refer to Chapter 2.

After the face has been smoothed, rotate the stock 90 degrees and pass the wood over the jointer to create two perpendicular surfaces.

Figure 11-1. Saw and joint two adjacent and perpendicular surfaces of the log or plank you intend to saw into veneers.

You may also need to rip the opposite side or edge on the band saw or table saw, creating a flat surface for the marking procedure that follows. Keep the veneers in sequential order throughout this process so they can be matched later. To accomplish that, mark the bottom edge of the board with some type of triangle or angled line pattern that can only be recreated by stacking the leaves in their original order. The pattern can also be drawn on one end of the board. Another way to keep the veneers in consecutive order is to number each leaf on its face immediately after cutting it. The first method is quicker and easier because you do not have to think about numbering while cutting and planing. To be totally safe, use both methods together. Note that numbering the edges of the veneers does not work—the numbers will disappear when you plane the leaves to their final thickness.

Before ripping the first sheet of veneer from the board on the band saw, you will need to make a line ⅛" in from the face along the top edge of the board, to use as a reference when cutting. It is easiest to use a marking gauge (**Figure 11-2**)

Figure 11-2. Use the marking gauge to scribe a line indicating the thickness of the first veneer you wish to saw.

because the operation will be repeated for each cut. A leaf that is ⅛" thick, or just a bit thinner, after one face has been smoothed on the jointer and ripped on the band saw, will leave just enough material to yield a finished thickness of about ¹⁄₁₆" after planing. One-eighth inch thick allows for a slight amount of error when sawing.

The rip fence

There are two types of rip fence to help guide the wood through the band saw accurately. The most common type, included with most band saws, resembles a table saw rip fence. It is essentially a straightedge secured parallel to the blade. The wood stays pressed against the fence as it is being cut. If you do not have the standard fence, you can clamp a board or straightedge to the saw table as a rip fence. The fence must be properly aligned with the blade and the blade must be sharp to get an accurate cut; otherwise, the cut can wander away from the line. If the blade does wander away from the intended path, the straightedge fence will prevent you from being able to steer the cut back in line.

The problem of wandering off the line, as well as burning of the wood, can be caused by a dull blade. A dull blade can also bend or belly inside the cut, causing cupped and bowed surfaces on the wood. The guide blocks and rollers on the band saw must also be properly aligned. The straightedge style of rip fence works well in most cases if these guidelines are addressed.

The point style of fence, which allows for the wood to be steered as it is being cut, is shown in **Figure 11-3**. The point of the fence must be aligned with the teeth of the band saw blade. It also helps to have the fence be as tall as the wood. This type of fence allows the wood to be steered back in line if the cut starts to wander.

Sawing the veneers

When using either type of fence, it is crucial to keep the wood firmly pressed against the fence from top to bottom, to prevent producing veneers thicker or thinner along one edge or the other. It also is important to feed the wood steadily and evenly. If everything is set up properly and the blade begins to burn or the cuts start to bow or cup anyway, it is time for a new blade. When beginning the cut, be careful to guide the blade right down the center of the scribed line (**Figure 11-4**).

As with any type of cut on a power machine, when the material gets too thin to hold or when nearing the end of a cut, use a push stick to protect your fingers. A board can split like a piece of firewood while being cut on a band saw, sending your fingers right into the blade. A push stick can prevent this.

After sawing the first sheet of veneer, set it aside and run the just-sawn face of the board over the jointer to smooth one face of the next leaf of veneer before you saw it. Repeat the process. If the jointer and band saw are close together and left running, the process can go quite fast.

For best results, do all of the cutting, jointing, and planing-to-thickness in one work session. There are several reasons for this. The veneer may dry unevenly, resulting in cupped and bowed sheets of veneer that will not go through the planer. Even if the cupped or bowed wood does go through the planer, it can emerge with uneven thicknesses across the width. Also, it is difficult to set the planer to exactly the same thickness twice, resulting in veneers of different thicknesses. Finally, the board itself may cup and bow if you leave it for several hours after sawing half of the veneers from it if the interior of the board is not as dry as the outer surfaces.

Figure 11-3. The point-style rip fence consists of a piece of plywood with a rounded edge, clamped to the band saw table a veneer thickness away from the blade. Two clamps are enough to stabilize the fence.

Figure 11-4. Start the cut with the wood pressed tightly against the band saw fence. Steer the cut by pivoting the wood on the fence.

Planing the veneers

When all of the veneer has been jointed on one side and sawn to ⅛" thickness, it is ready for the thickness planer. The material is difficult to run through the planer by itself without damaging it. If the planer has rollers on the bed (lower table), the thin material will not stay pressed down firmly. If the material is unsupported under the cutters, it will cut unevenly, split, tear, or even disintegrate entirely. I have seen veneer go in one side of the planer and never come out—the thin material breaks apart and goes up the chip chute.

There are several ways to avoid the problem, allowing many types of veneer to be planed down to 1/16" or even thinner. A backing board can help to keep veneer pressed down firmly throughout the cutting process. Two types of backing boards are commonly used to plane down veneer: one that does not travel through the machine with the veneer, and one that does.

The non-traveling type of backing board is usually surfaced with Melamine or some other smooth material over which the veneer can easily slide. The material for the backing board is cut to the width of the planer bed and slightly longer. A cleat is fastened under one end to prevent the backing board from traveling through the planer with the veneer. The planer's bed rollers are lowered below the table surface so the backing board rests firmly on the table. The veneer is fed into the planer one sheet at a time (**Figure 11-5**). It would be easy to feed several leaves through

Figure 11-5. A non-traveling backing board has a cleat on the infeed edge that catches on the infeed table. Feed the veneer one piece at a time.

Figure 11-6. A traveling backer board, faced with sandpaper to keep the veneer in place, travels through the planer with the veneer.

Band Sawing Veneers

Band-sawn veneers are thicker than manufactured ones, but with carefully tuned small-shop machinery you should be able to produce consistent veneers about 1/16" thick. The method is:

- Choose the surface of the plank or log you wish to have as veneer and joint it flat and smooth.
- Saw and joint a right-angled surface you can guide on the table of the band saw.
- Mount a point fence just ahead of the band saw teeth, about ⅛" away.
- Slice the first veneer from the plank or log. It will have one smooth surface and one sawn surface.
- Joint the sawn surface of the plank or log to make it smooth again.
- Saw the second veneer. Continue the joint-saw sequence until all of the veneers have been cut.
- Use a backing board to pass each leaf of veneer through the thickness planer and remove the band saw marks. Take several light cuts to reduce the thickness of the leaf to 1/16".

the planer side-by-side at the same time. If veneer is fed into the planer in this way, it can catch, slip, and bind, leaving burn marks and risking serious damage. Feeding each leaf into the planer at a slightly different side-to-side location relative to the cutter prevents damage and ensures uniform wear on the knives.

The traveling type of backing board, which passes through the planer with the veneer, seems to work even better but may take a little longer to use. The backing board needs to be uniform in thickness and slightly larger than the veneer. In addition, it should be made of a material with a rough surface to prevent the veneer from slipping as it passes through the planer. Fine sandpaper applied with contact adhesive to the surface of the backing board will eliminate slippage and keep the veneer well secured as it is cut (**Figure 11-6**).

Accomplishing the planing step in one or two passes is beneficial: The fewer passes through the planer, the less chance there is for something to go wrong. To avoid a rough surface, however, not more than 1/16" of material should ever be removed in one pass.

Storing the veneer

After being planed down to the finished thickness, the veneer needs to be stored to allow air to reach all sides evenly. If too much moisture escapes from one side of the veneer relative to the other side, the veneer can cup, twist, bow, and then crack when glued down or pressed down flat. Even if a board appears to be dry, the moisture content deep inside will be different than that near the surface. There also might be tensions within the wood that will only appear when the wood is cut apart. Narrow strips of wood, or stickers, need to be placed across the grain and stacked with the veneer (**Figure 11-7**). Allowing the veneer to dry in this manner for 24 hours should be enough time for it to stabilize properly. Once the leaves have been sawn, planed, and dried, shop-cut veneers can be used like any other veneer.

Grain Orientation

The orientation of the grain relative to the cutters has a large impact on the quality of the surface that emerges from the planer or jointer, which is particularly important when making veneer. For best results, the long grain of the wood should feed squarely into the planer knives. As the knives cut through the wood, they should shear off the wood fibers cleanly, not pull and rip the fibers out. When you plane veneer cross grain or diagonally to the grain, the fibers can easily be pulled completely out to the other side, leaving holes through the veneer. The smoothest possible veneer with the largest yield per board can be achieved if the grain direction is properly considered, the knives are sharp, and both the cutter head and feed rate are adjusted properly.

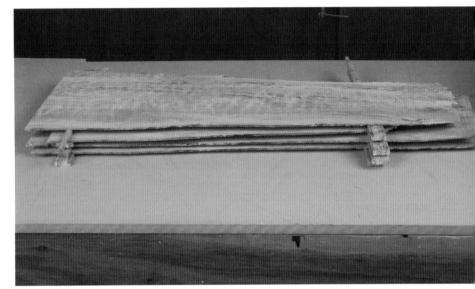

Figure 11-7. Sticker the veneers so air can circulate all around each leaf—they need to acclimate and stabilize.

CHAPTER 12

Mirror Frame

To demonstrate the basic skills necessary to create a bent lamination using veneers in a small project, using only clamps to press the veneer, a curved mirror frame is a good project to detail. The curved frame pieces consist of a face veneer bonded to bendable MDF and bending plywood inner layers. The edges will be finished by hammer veneering.

While you could make the frame using any of the pressing techniques described in Chapter 6, I will detail how to accomplish this by using clamps, cauls, and a two-part, shop-made bending form. Hammer veneering is also discussed in Chapter 6.

Here is the completed mirror project detailed in this chapter.

Full-size drawing

For most projects, I make a full-size drawing. Many of my pieces are symmetrical. If you draw a line through the center of the design, it is the same on both sides, much like a mirror image. I often draw only one side because the other side is identical (**Figure 12-1**).

Complex curves are difficult enough to draw even once. They can be drawn using a compass; a curved object, such as a can or a bucket; a thin flexible stick; or a French curve. They also can be drawn freehand (as I often do) and then refined. An accurate, full-size drawing is important. The drawing is used to trace the shape of the curve for making the bending form and acts as a pattern upon which you can place the pieces of the project at various times during construction. Once your drawing is complete, lay some transparent tracing paper over the curve, tape it in place with drafting tape, and trace the curve.

Figure 12-1. Make a full-size, simple drawing. This drawing shows the front elevation and the side view of one side of the mirror frame.

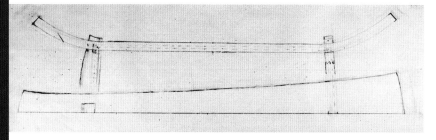

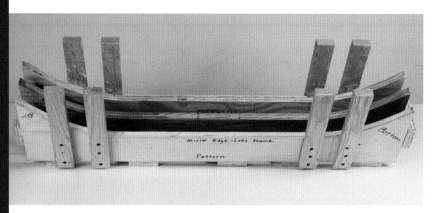

Figure 12-2. The ribs of the bending form should be about an inch apart. The vertical pieces are locating posts that will mate with the top half of the jig.

Bending jig

The mirror project can be built using a half-dozen sturdy clamps and a two-part form constructed out of plywood or MDF. To be able to make this two-part form with the proper curve, we need to consider how the bending jig will be constructed. A bending jig usually is made of vertical ribs spaced about one inch apart with some type of structure to hold them in place (**Figure 12-2**). The ribs need to be covered with some type of pad or blanket, usually made of ¼" or ⅜" bending plywood, spanning the distance between them and creating a smooth, uniform surface.

To determine the exact radius of the curves to be cut into the ribs, we need to add up the thickness of the finished workpiece, as well as the thickness of both blankets. Otherwise, the radius of the top and bottom of the form will not match up, resulting in gaps within the finished panel. For the mirror project, the blankets are each ⅜" thick, and the laminated sides themselves will add up to ⅞", for a total distance of 1⅝" between the top and bottom halves of the bending form. The blankets need not be attached to the form. They can be set in loose, along with the veneer panels, during glue-up.

If you plan to use a vacuum bag press instead of clamps and cauls, you will need only the convex side of the form. The construction of that side will be the same as the process described below. Be certain the form is sturdy and there are no air pockets inside, or it is liable to collapse inside the vacuum bag.

Make the Ribs

Saw a pattern rib first; then, saw and rout the rest of the ribs to exactly follow the shape of the first rib. Use a straight cutter with a bearing on the shaft in the router table (**Figure 12-3**). This method is particularly useful in making forms for wide panels because they require many identical ribs. Make every laminated panel about 1" longer

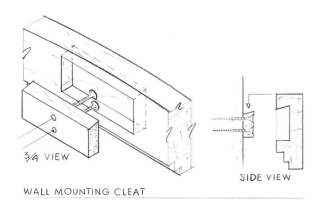

3/4 VIEW

SIDE VIEW

WALL MOUNTING CLEAT

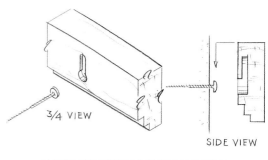

3/4 VIEW

SIDE VIEW

ALTERNATE KEYHOLE SLOT MOUNTING

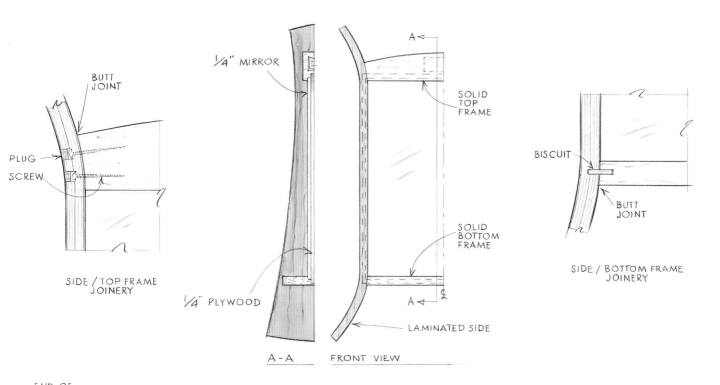

BUTT JOINT

PLUG

SCREW

SIDE / TOP FRAME JOINERY

1/4" MIRROR

1/4" PLYWOOD

A-A

FRONT VIEW

A

SOLID TOP FRAME

SOLID BOTTOM FRAME

LAMINATED SIDE

A

BISCUIT

BUTT JOINT

SIDE / BOTTOM FRAME JOINERY

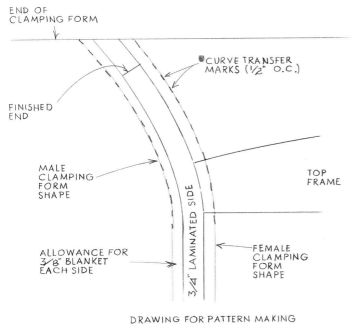

END OF CLAMPING FORM

CURVE TRANSFER MARKS (1/2" O.C.)

FINISHED END

MALE CLAMPING FORM SHAPE

3/4" LAMINATED SIDE

TOP FRAME

ALLOWANCE FOR 3/8" BLANKET EACH SIDE

FEMALE CLAMPING FORM SHAPE

DRAWING FOR PATTERN MAKING

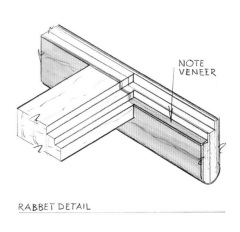

NOTE VENEER

RABBET DETAIL

Illustrations by Mike Bray.

Figure 12-3. Cut the straight sections of the bending form ribs on the table saw before pattern-routing the curves using a straight bit with a bearing on its shaft.

than it needs to be, both to allow for any slipping during the gluing process and to make a good clean cut at each end later. Add the extra length to the pattern rib when laying it out. For the same reasons, when measuring the panel width, I usually add at least ¼" on each edge.

Lay out the pattern rib and use a band saw or a jig saw to cut it out, staying as close to the line as possible. Smooth the cut surface using a file, spindle sander, disk sander, belt sander, or sandpaper. Remember, the rest of the ribs will match the pattern exactly, so take time to get it as smooth as possible. Now, the pattern can be used to create the rest of the ribs, by sawing just outside the line and pattern-routing to the precise shape.

Assemble the Bending Jig

To assemble the bending jig, attach the ribs together with plywood (Figure 12-2). Place 1"-thick spacer blocks between each rib during assembly. The blocks either can be removed or left in place upon completion. The plywood pieces that join the ribs can be 4" to 5" apart, but there must be enough material near each end of the form to prevent flexing.

Finally, you need guides to keep the two parts of the form from sliding around while clamping

(Figure 12-2). If the guides are made of oak or some other hardwood, the form can be reused many times. The guide strips need to be at least 1" wide so they don't split when screwed to the form. I usually make four sets of three strips the length of the height of the form when it is under pressure. For each set of three, attach the two outer strips to the bottom of the form and attach the center strip to the upper half of the form. Place a piece of veneer between each pair of strips during construction. Remove it afterward. Doing so allows just enough room to open and close the form without any slipping. In addition, place the sets of three strips at different locations on each side of the form. The strip placement will allow only one way for the form to go together during the heat of gluing up.

After assembling the form, rub all of the interior surfaces, including the guides, with paraffin or candle wax. The wax lubricates the surfaces for easy separation and prevents any excess glue from bonding the form closed.

Prepare and glue the face veneer

Now, prepare both the surface veneer and the laminate material for gluing. Many types of flexible sheet material can be used for the interior laminates, including most species of ⅛" plywood, ⅛" MDF, lauan bender board, or a combination thereof. In almost every case, when constructing a curved panel with a veneered surface, I glue up the curve in two steps. The first step is to glue the surface veneer down flat to one interior laminate. The first step creates a semi-rigid outer shell with veneer that won't slide or buckle during the final gluing process. The second step is to combine all of the layers together in the curved form and then to glue them together. Any defects caused by slight irregularities in the form, uneven clamp pressure, or shifting of the layers during clamping, are buried in the center of the panel and hidden from view.

I usually use ⅛" MDF for the outer layer because it provides a firm, sturdy, and void-free surface, which makes the panel feel like solid wood when touched or tapped.

For step one, make three cauls of ¾" particleboard or plywood slightly larger than the veneers. Two pieces of thick stock to use as cauls between the clamps and the bending form help distribute the pressure (**Figure 12-4**).

If all of the sheets of face veneer match, create a left and right mirror frame based on the veneer's figure pattern. Take the time to align and mark the veneer properly to avoid confusion during the glue-up. Spread glue on one side of each of the ⅛" MDF pieces with a notched trowel. Remember to apply glue only to the laminate, not to the veneer. Otherwise, it will curl up before you can press it down. Also, spritz a little distilled water or commercial veneer softener onto the top surface of the veneer, just after placing it on the glue.

Titebond Extend or Titebond III glues allow at least 10 minutes of open time to get everything lined up and clamped. Tighten the center clamps first, allowing the veneer to flatten out as the glue and wrinkles gradually work their way toward the ends. Wait one or two minutes, then tighten the outer clamps. Allow the veneer and the laminates to dry for an hour. Remove the clamps and move on to the bending process while the glue is still somewhat flexible.

Bending the panels

Combine the blankets, face veneers, and interior plies in the bending form with glue, and tighten the clamps. Leave it overnight to cure.

All of the laminates can now be combined in the curved form. Place the appropriate blankets on the bottom half of the form with a piece of clean newsprint for protection. Spread the glue using the notched trowel as before, but apply glue to both sides of each center laminate. Once the stack is complete, drive a ¾" screw into the

Figure 12-4. The surface veneers are being glued to ⅛" MDF. Thick MDF cauls and straight pieces of wood distribute the clamping pressure. Both surface veneers can be glued at one time, face to face between the cauls.

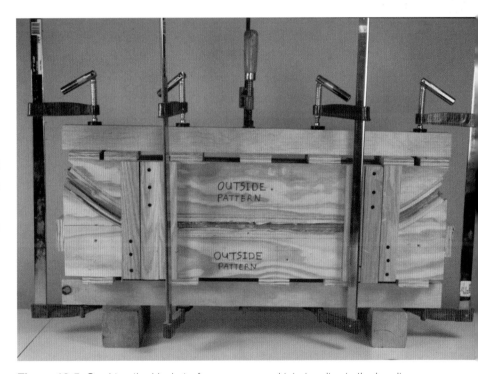

Figure 12-5. Combine the blankets, face veneers, and interior plies in the bending form with glue. Tighten the clamps and leave it overnight to cure.

Figure 12-6. Rough-cut one edge of the glue-up by band sawing. Straighten it on the table saw using a push stick to complete the cut. Please note: The guard was removed to show the cuts. Do not remove the guard from your tool.

Figure 12-7. The mirror sides have a tapered shape, as indicated by the paper pattern taped onto the lamination.

length of the workpiece, parallel to the line you want to be your finished edge.

Cut carefully along this line with a band saw, jigsaw, or handsaw. Clean up this edge with a hand plane or sandpaper; then, saw the final edge on the table saw (**Figure 12-6**). If you are not comfortable making the cut on the table saw, or if the radius of your curve is too large to fit on the table saw, just band saw and plane or sand the finished edge straight.

Shaping the Curved Edges

To make only one of a particular design, I make a pattern using tracing paper that can either be taped right onto the workpiece with double-stick transparent tape or fastened with removable spray-type contact adhesive. For multiples of a design, I make a pattern of ⅛" MDF, which will bend as needed when I'm drawing around it. Attach the drawing or trace a line on each panel (**Figure 12-7**), and then use a band saw or jigsaw to saw it.

Do not cut the ends to length yet. The hammer veneering process is difficult right at the end of a curve. The extra material gives you some room to work. Trim the ends clean when you are done hammer veneering. Before removing waste, it is important to think ahead about where that waste will be and how it could be used.

With the line or tracing paper still in place, use a fine rasp, coarse file, or sandpaper to smooth out any irregularities. If you wish to have a flat

border or waste area of the panel to keep the laminates from sliding around.

Place newsprint and blankets on top, and then put the form together. Place the thick clamping beams on the top and bottom of the form. Clamp as shown in **Figure 12-5**. Apply pressure in the center first, before applying pressure to the ends. Doing so forces any irregularities, imperfections, and excess glue out the ends. Allow the glue to cure overnight before releasing the clamp to greatly reduce any springback, or relaxation, of the curve.

Straightening the Edges

Now that the bent-laminated sides of the mirror frame have been glued up and dried, they can be cut, shaped, and prepared for hammer veneering the edges. Begin by establishing one straight edge on the lamination, before cutting any curves. Use a flexible ruler or a piece of bendable wood to draw a straight line in the waste area along the

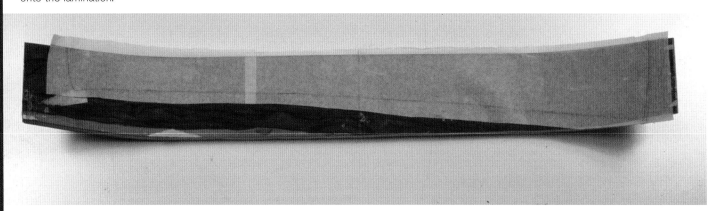

edge on your finished piece, skip the next step and go directly to hammer veneering. I prefer a bull-nosed edge, which nicely complements the other curves in the design. While the bull nose could be shaped on the router table, it's tricky with curved pieces. I just round the edge using a spokeshave, rasp, and Surform (**Figure 12-8**) and then finish it using 80- and 120-grit sandpaper. The process provides a smooth, uniform surface suitable for hammer veneering.

Preparing the edge veneer

Once you have formed the edges of the panel, whether flat or bull nosed, you are ready to cover the edges with veneer. I use ordinary yellow PVA glue or Titebond II glue for this process and will show you how to hammer down the veneer.

For the mirror project, I had an extra leaf of veneer from the same flitch that exactly matched the veneer on the surface. Having the leaf allowed me to create the illusion of a single solid board. If it is your first attempt at hammer veneering, I recommend trying out the process on scraps of plywood, using the same veneer you plan to use for this project.

Stand the curved mirror side on edge on the veneer to be used for the bull nose. Trace a line about ½" wider than the curve on all sides (**Figure 12-9**). Use a sharp knife to cut the veneer, being careful not to pull it apart.

With the veneer cut out, spread a thin layer of PVA glue on its underside and spray a little distilled water on the top to prevent it from curling up. Spread a thin layer of glue on the edge of the workpiece. Allow the glue to dry long enough for a skin to form over the top. The glue is ready and at its most flexible when it turns from a creamy white color to dark yellow in color, and when your finger will slide right over the surface of the glue without sticking. Then it is dry enough to remelt easily without making a mess, yet moist enough to help ease the veneer around the curves.

Figure 12-8. Shape a bull nose on the edge of the mirror frame using either a Surform rasp or a spokeshave, and sandpaper.

Figure 12-9. Trace the mirror side onto the veneer you will use to cover the bull-nose edge. Make the tracing ½" extra wide all around.

Figure 12-10. Lay the veneer onto the edge and heat a section of it with the iron.

Figure 12-11. Use the veneer hammer to press the heated veneer onto the curved edge.

Hammer veneering the edge

With a hot electric iron and a veneer hammer ready, the veneer can be applied. Clamp the panel securely on edge, either in a vise or to a bench, arranged so you can work on one end and the two sides at the same time. Place the veneer, glue-side down, over the edge to be covered. Make sure it is centered—the same amount of veneer should overhang each side; otherwise, there will not be enough material to fully cover both sides of the bull-nose curve.

Start at one end of the panel, applying heat with the iron to the veneer at the top, or crown, of the bull nose. Heat an area about 6" long, until the glue starts to bubble, as shown in **Figure 12-10**. If the veneer starts to brown, or even burn a little, the discoloration can be sanded off later.

Once this area is heated, quickly remove the iron and start to apply pressure with the veneer hammer (**Figure 12-11**). Hold the head of the veneer hammer with one hand, and hold the veneer in place with the other hand. Move the hammer back and forth over the area that was heated, applying as much pressure as possible,

until the glue has cooled significantly. There should now be a bond between the veneer and the workpiece. Make sure there is a good bond in each area before moving on to the next area—if the veneer continues to slide around on the surface, apply more heat and try again.

Working the Curved Edge

Once you have achieved a proper bond along the top of the curve, start to round over one side of the veneer for the same distance as you just covered (**Figure 12-12**). Start on either side of the workpiece. I usually do it in two steps, first working about halfway down from top of the curve, getting that bonded, and then hammer veneering the bottom of the bull nose. Don't worry about that last little bit at the very edge. It will be finished later, when the excess veneer is trimmed.

Go back over the whole face of the curve with the iron and the hammer, smoothing the veneer and securing any small loose spots. To check for loose spots, tap the surface of the veneer with your fingernail. If you hear the deep sound of solid wood, there is a good bond. If you hear a hollow

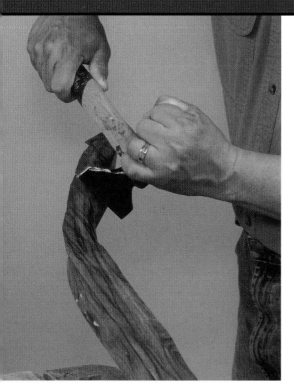

Figure 12-12. Work the iron and the veneer hammer around the curved edge. Most veneers are flexible enough to follow a curve like this without cracking.

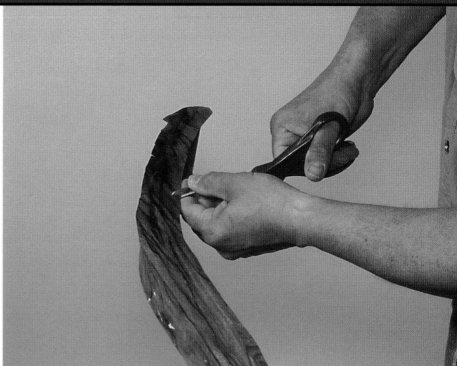

Figure 12-13. Use scissors to snip into the waste area of the veneer, to help work it over the bull nose.

scratching sound, go back over that spot with the hot iron and then the veneer hammer. When touching up small spots, just use the tip of the iron.

At this point, you should have the crown and one face of the bull-nose curve glued down tight along the first 6" to 8" of the panel. Next, hammer veneer the other face of the bull-nose curve. The veneer should be flexible enough to conform to the curve. In most cases, the heat from the iron and the moisture from remelting the glue is enough to stretch the veneer around the curve.

In some areas of a curve, the veneer might need to stretch or compress to conform to a shape. In such cases, make a few cuts into the waste area of the veneer to relieve the stress (**Figure 12-13**). Be careful not to cut into the area of the veneer that will remain. If the veneer won't conform, it might be too brittle (see Troubleshooting, at right).

Keep on Hammering

Once the entire radius of the bull-nose curve has been covered for 6" to 8", repeat the process as you move down the length of the curve. As you are working on the two faces of the curve, notice

Troubleshooting

If the veneer is sliding around on the surface after heating and hammering, and will not adhere, there could be a couple of reasons.

Check to make sure enough glue was applied and allowed to dry for the appropriate length of time. The glue should completely cover the surface, without creating any pools. Glue cannot adhere until the excess has been boiled away. With pools of glue, by the time the iron has boiled the excess away, either the glue on the other surface has long since disappeared or the veneer has become too burned up and dried out to use.

New glue can be applied with a little strip of veneer, by pushing the veneer under the surface in the dried-out area. You can also force a little glue into the area with your fingertip. Once the new glue has been allowed to dry, the area can be heated and pressed down with the hammer again. Be careful not to heat up any adjacent areas that did bond properly to avoid remelting and loosening up the glue there.

Glue not allowed to dry long enough also will allow movement of the veneer. Because PVA glue is thermoplastic, if not allowed to dry long enough, it can actually sit on the surface for days before it is bonded. Remember, veneer is at its most flexible just after the glue skins over.

Unfortunately, some veneers are just too brittle to conform to any curve without breaking apart. That's why it is essential to try hammer veneering any new species of veneer onto the edge of a scrap of curved wood before committing it to a project.

Figure 12-14. Trim the excess veneer with a sharp chisel.

veneer guides the blade away from the workpiece. If the cut follows the grain into the panel, it is easy to tear the veneer off. You might have to change directions several times along the curve. I usually trim about 10" at a time. I stop and look for gaps in the glue line where the face veneer and the edge veneer come together. I then reheat and hammer-veneer just that small area where they join, creating a nice, tight seam.

Before you can trim the last ¹⁄₁₆" of waste veneer, the ends of the panel need to be cut to their final size and shape and hammer veneered. For the mirror design, I decided to cut the ends of the panel to a gentle curve with a flat profile. The treatment continues the illusion of a solid board. It is very difficult to veneer a corner where two bull-nose edges come together. In fact, it is difficult to hammer veneer right out to the end of any edge that has a bull-nose curve.

Because I left the panel long on each end, it can be easily sawn to the finished size. The flat end can be covered with veneer—the veneer won't have to conform to a compound curve.

how the veneer seems to pull away at the far end of the workpiece. While you are working on one face, it pulls away from the center of the crown in that direction. On the other face it pulls away in the other direction. Keep an eye on it as you progress along the curve.

I usually continue to test the position of the veneer, forming it over the curve just ahead of where I am hammer veneering. Continue working small areas until you reach the end of the curve. Reposition the workpiece in the vise as needed to apply maximum pressure where you are working.

Trimming excess veneer

With the edge veneer applied, I prefer to trim and seal up any small gaps near the edge right away, before the glue gets too dried out. There are several ways to trim excess veneer. I use a chisel (**Figure 12-14**), with the back of the blade riding on the panel. A thin, flexible knife also trims well. Either way, work along the length of the curve and pare all but about ¹⁄₁₆" of the excess veneer from each edge. The excess will be removed later.

Keep track of the grain direction in the veneer, and work in the direction where the grain of the

Final trimming and sanding

Once all of the edges have been covered and trimmed, I use a steel scraper blade with a burr to scrape the last of the waste veneer from the side of the panel. I also scrape any glue residue off the surface of the entire panel to prepare it for finish sanding. As with the chisel, scrape by following the grain direction of the edge veneer away from the panel to shear the fibers off cleanly. Sand either by using a random orbit sander with 220-grit sandpaper or by hand.

It is usually best to sand the panel before fitting anything to it. It can be very frustrating to get all of the parts of a project to fit just right, only to see that nice, tight fit destroyed by finish sanding. I go over the veneered surfaces to clean up everything, sanding lightly by hand with 220-grit sandpaper, just prior to finishing.

Completing the frame

With the side panels of the mirror completed, we can move on to making the top and bottom of the mirror frame. The parts could take any shape, but I like to incorporate curves to create unity with the curved sides. Solid wood is a good choice because it is sturdy enough for anchoring the sides and can be milled flat where it meets the flat mirror.

Place the frame members on the full-size drawing to get all of the angles and curves just right. If you don't have a completed drawing, place the parts on a piece of ⅛" plywood and trace around them. The process is a good method for working quickly and freely because you can change and measure things easily. Once everything is right where you want it, draw around all of the parts, taking exact measurements and angles off the drawing whenever you need them.

Frame joints

Butt joints are the simplest way to fasten the horizontal pieces to the curved mirror sides. The top is anchored to the laminated sides with screws, using decorative plugs to cap the screw heads. The screws anchor into solid wood; however, strength is not a main consideration because the ¼" plywood back will add both strength and stability to the frame.

I made the bottom of the frame into a little shelf for keys, sunglasses, or makeup. The shelf joins the side frame members where they curve. Because this is a gentle curve and the area of contact is short, I cut the end of the shelf to the proper angle with a miter saw, taking the angle off the drawing. The shelf can be joined to the sides using screws, biscuits, or dowels. I chose biscuits, so nothing would be exposed on the outside of the frame.

Rabbetting the frame

When all of the corners fit neatly, place a clamp across the top and bottom of the frame to ensure everything is tight and square. I made the corner blocks and clamped up the frame (**Figure 12-15**). If everything looks good, turn the entire frame over to mark the rabbets for the mirror and the back.

Use ¼"-thick mirror glass—⅛" mirror glass bends and distorts when placed in a frame. I used ¼" plywood for the back: It is thin enough to work with the wood thicknesses in this design but thick enough to add support and stability. Lay out the rabbets with two steps (**Figure 12-16**). The mirror rabbet will be ½" deep, to allow for the thickness of both the mirror and the plywood. The plywood rabbet will be ⅜" wider on each side, to make room for anchoring the screws that hold the back in place. If you made the side members ⅞" thick, there will be plenty of room.

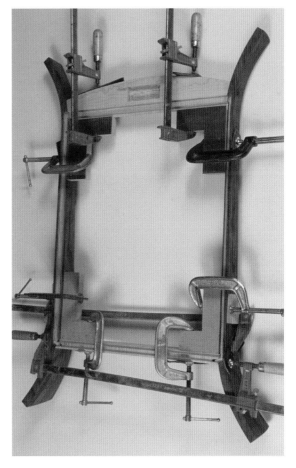

Figure 12-15. Clamp up the mirror frame dry, using blocks to help keep the parts square to one another.

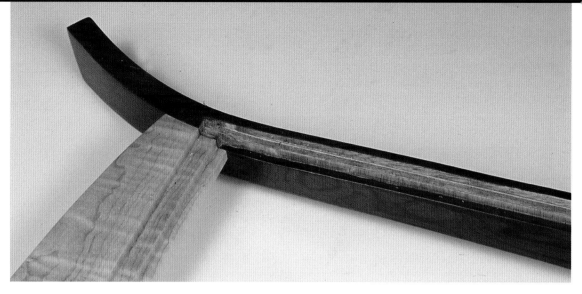

Figure 12-16. The mirror frame has a double rabbet, one step for the mirror glass and the other for the plywood back.

Figure 12-17. Because the bottom of the rabbet reflects in the mirror, it must be veneered to match the side pieces.

Lay out and rout the rabbets. Make clearly visible marks on the frame where the rabbets begin and end, so you know when to start and stop the cuts.

Make the depth of the mirror rabbet in the side frames deeper, by the thickness of one veneer, than the thickness of the mirror itself. You will need to hammer veneer the bottom of the rabbet because once the mirror is in place you will see the reflection of the little surface in the edge of the glass (**Figure 12-17**). If you are painting the edges of the frame, you can paint this edge as well. The back of the frame sides can be left uncovered, hammer veneered, or painted.

Constructing the hanger

To provide for hanging the mirror, mill a slot into the top piece of the mirror frame (Figure 12-15), with a mating cleat of wood mounted on the wall. Doing so creates a strong and safe way to secure the mirror to the wall, while keeping it easy to hang.

Make the slot 1¼" wide by 3¼" long by ½" deep. I cut it on the router table, but it could be done using a plunge router. To finish the mortise and create an angle that will act as a hook for the mirror to hang on, use a dovetail bit in the

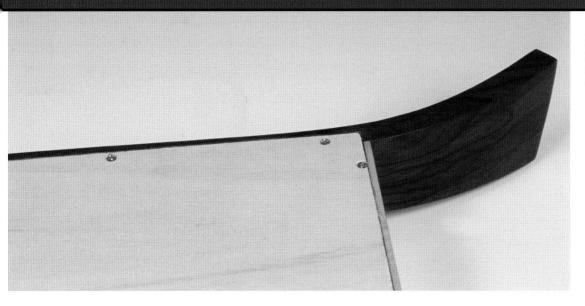

router table. Then, mill a cleat to mount on the wall, beveled at the same angle as the dovetail bit. Make the cleat slightly thinner than the depth of the mortise and slightly shorter than its length.

Assembling the frame

With all of the rabbets cut, pre-assemble and clamp the frame with all of the appropriate screws, dowels, or biscuits in place. Square up all the corners of the rabbets with a sharp chisel. Make sure everything is square and the rabbets all match up. The mirror rabbets should form a flat ledge all the way around the frame. If there are any irregularities in the rabbet, the mirror will crack when you tighten down the plywood back (**Figure 12-18**). Now, disassemble the frame and, if you did not already do so, hammer veneer the bottom of the mirror rabbet on the side frames.

Once everything has been completed and sanded, it's best to assemble the mirror frame without glue one more time to be certain everything fits properly. Drop the mirror into place to make sure it fits. The mirror frame should now be ready to glue up.

For the mirror frame, I glued up and sanded everything before applying the finish. If I had decided to mask and paint the edges, I would probably have done most of the finishing before gluing up. One final note: When applying the back of the mirror frame with screws, place acid-free paper between the back of the mirror and the plywood to protect the reflective coating on the back of the glass.

The mirror frame project is a good way to learn the basics of creating a curved panel and finishing off the edge. Being able to use curves can give your work a new sense of freedom, creating design possibilities you might never have imagined.

Appendix 1

Glossary

Banding. Lines of veneer inlaid into a veneer field is called banding. Banding is normally taped to the field veneers before pressing.

Bending form. A wooden mold, made in one part for vacuum bag pressing and two parts for use with clamps and screws, is a bending form and presses veneers and suitable substrates together to take on the curve of the mold.

Book-match. Leaves of veneer joined so the front side of one sheet butts to the back of the next, like the pages of a book, are book-matched.

Border. Veneers cut to fit around a central field are borders. Many veneered panels need a border to appear complete.

Caul. A flat piece of wood or one with a bowed center, helps distribute clamping pressure across a veneered panel. The caul also keeps the press screws from direct contact with the delicate veneer.

Clamping beam. A heavy wooden caul used to distribute pressure across a veneer glue-up is a clamping beam.

Clip, clipped. The process of straightening the long edges of veneer leaves is called clipping.

Coping saw. A U-shaped saw frame with a wooden handle, which takes standard pin-end blades, is a coping saw. Can be used to saw veneers and thin wood in intricate shapes.

Crossband. Veneer laid under the face veneer and at right angles to it, to stabilize the panel and improve the adhesion of the face veneers to the substrate or ground, is called crossband veneer or counter-veneer.

Cross-grain lamination. Cross-grain lamination is made up of thin layers of wood, with their grain direction running at 90 degrees from layer to layer.

Double-bevel sawing. A shape sawn from two layers of veneer with the saw held at an angle of about 15 degrees, so the top piece will drop into the cutout in the bottom piece with no gaps, is called double-bevel sawing.

Dry-glue defects. Voids or bubbles under veneer caused by too little glue or improper adhesion are dry-glue defects. Remedy by adding new glue and pressing the defect flat.

Field. The background veneer in a veneered panel with a border or inlay is called the field.

Flitch cut. Flitch cutting is slicing the veneer from a log along its length or from a slab (like peeling a carrot).

Flitch. A stack of veneer sheets sliced from the log and kept in sequential order, so the grain and figure match from one leaf to the next, is called a flitch.

Four-way match. Four successive leaves of veneer arranged around a central point, with the wood figure reflected right to left and top to bottom is known as a four-way match.

Hot press. An industrial veneer press used to set glue very quickly is called a hot press. It has heated platens, a radio-frequency heating apparatus, or both.

Inlay. A veneer motif, medallion, or band let into a precisely fitted recess cut into a larger veneered or solid-wood surface, with the surface finishing level, is an inlay.

Jeweler's saw. An adjustable saw frame with a pin vise at each end that can accept extremely fine blades is a jeweler's saw. Can make a finer cut than a coping saw.

Kerf. The width of a saw cut, which in veneer work must be compensated for in some way, is called a kerf. When setting an inlay into a veneer field, sawing the opening would create a kerf and would require the inlay to be made correspondingly larger to fill the kerf.

Lamination, laminate, delaminate. Layers of wood glued together are called laminae or laminates. The assembled panel is called a lamination. If the layers should become unglued and separate, they are said to have delaminated.

Layup, laying up. A layup is assembly of veneer pieces fit neatly together and held in place by veneer tape.

Leaf, leaves. Sheets of veneer are also called leaves.

Marquetry. Marquetry is the art of cutting and assembling small pieces of veneer into pictures.

Medium-Density Fiberboard. Medium-density fiberboard, or MDF, is a man-made material composed of wood chips and glue, with a uniform texture and a firm surface layer. MDF is an ideal substrate for veneer.

Parquetry. The art of cutting and assembling small pieces of veneer into geometric patterns is parquetry.

Particleboard. A man-made material consisting of coarser particles than MDF, particleboard is usually not suitable for veneering.

Plywood. Hardwood plywood is a man-made material consisting of many thin layers or laminations of wood glued together, with the grain in the wood running crosswise from layer to layer. Plywood is a good substrate for veneer. Most plywood has an odd number of layers.

Pressure fan, pressure cone. Pressure from a clamp or veneer screw fans out in a 45-degree cone from the point of application—this is called a pressure fan. Inserting a thick caul between the screw and the workpiece helps distribute the pressure.

Radial match. When triangles of identical veneer are fit together to make a circle, a radial match is made. A radial match commonly has 8, 12, or 16 veneer points.

Rotary cut. Using a sharp knife to peel the veneer from a round log, similar to paper towels unrolling, is rotary cutting. The process is used mostly to manufacture plywood from crosswise layers of veneers and is used to cover large plywood and MDF panels with decorative veneers.

Sand shading. Shading light-colored veneers by scorching them in hot sand is called sand shading. This technique is used for marquetry pictures.

Sawing table. A small work platform mounted on a raised stake, on which marquetry pieces can be sawn, is a sawing table. It's also called a bird's mouth because of the deep V usually cut into the table.

Sizing. Sizing means filling the pores of the veneer with a water-soluble chemical mixture, typically including glycerin or an adhesive, to help keep it flat.

Slip-match. Leaves of veneer joined so all the sheets are in order and facing the same side out, repeating the figure pattern across the panel, are slip-matched.

Springback. The tendency of bent wood, including glued-up bent laminations, to give up some of their curvature upon being released from a bending form is known as spring back.

Substrate. The substrate is the base panel on which veneers may be glued. To avoid warping, the substrate must be veneered on both sides, not just one. Traditional substrates were made of solid wood, often sawn into narrow strips. Contemporary substrates most often are made of plywood or medium-density fiberboard.

Tape, taping. Taping describes the process of using veneer tape, a paper-based material, to hold pieces of veneer together in a layup. Most veneering projects require some amount of taping.

Veneer hammer. A hand tool used to squeegee veneer down tight is a veneer hammer. The tool usually is used in conjunction with a hot iron that melts the glue.

Veneer punch. A sharp cutting tool, or veneer punch, removes a circle or an irregular shape from veneer in order to cut out a small defect and make way for a patch cut with the same tool.

Wet-glue defects. Bulges in glued veneer caused by too much glue, called wet-glue defects, can be remedied by forcing excess glue out of the veneer.

Wood grain, grain pattern. Long fibers that make up wood are the wood grain. Grain runs in the direction of the tree trunk, but it can also run toward a cut surface, "with the grain," or away from it, "against the grain." Grain is a factor in how wood appears.

Wood figure, figure pattern. The wood figure is the appearance of wood influenced by knots, straightness of the tree trunk, color changes between heartwood and sapwood, stains caused by minerals and chemicals in the wood, and marks made by weather, insects, or other trauma throughout the tree's life.

Appendix 2

Index

Appendix 2 *(continued)*

Appendix 3

Veneering Suppliers

A & M Wood Specialty
357 Eagle Street North
P.O. Box 32040
Cambridge, ON N3H 5M2
Canada
(519) 653-9322
1-800-265-2759
www.forloversofwood.com
Thick veneers

B&B Rare Woods
4581 South Queen Street
Littleton, CO 80127
(303) 986-2585
www.wood-veneers.com
Veneer

Certainly Wood
13000 Route 78
East Aurora, NY 14052-9515
(716) 655-0206
www.certainlywood.com
Veneer

Erath Veneers
160 Industrial Avenue
P.O. Box 507
Rocky Mount, VA 24151
www.erathveneer.com
Veneer

Hearne Hardwoods
200 Whiteside Drive
Oxford, PA 19363
1-888-814-0007
www.hearnehardwoods.com

Highland Woodworking
1045 North Highland Avenue Northeast
Atlanta, GA 30306
1-800-241-6748
www.highlandwoodworking.com
Veneering supplies

Lee Valley & Veritas
P.O. Box 1780
Ogdensburg, NY 13669-6780
1-800-871-8158
www.leevalley.com
Veneering supplies

Oakwood Veneer Company
1830 Stephenson Highway
Troy, MI 48083
1-800-426-6018
www.oakwoodveneer.com
Paper-backed veneer sheets

Rockler Woodworking and Hardware
4365 Willow Drive
Medina, MN 55340
1-800-233-9359
www.rockler.com
Veneering supplies

Treefrog Veneer
39 O'Neil Street
Easthampton, MA 01027
1-800-830-5448
www.treefrogveneer.com
Made-made veneers

Vacuum Pressing Systems
553 River Road
Brunswick, ME 04011
1-800-382-4109
www.vacupress.com
Vacuum press and veneering supplies

Veneer Systems Inc.
100 River Rock Drive
Suite 104
Buffalo, NY 14207
1-800-825-0840
www.veneersystems.com
Vacuum press and veneering supplies

Woodcraft Stores
1-800-225-1153
www.woodcraft.com
Veneering supplies and some veneer

Woodsmith Store
10320 Hickman Road
Des Moines, IA 50325
(515) 254-9494
www.woodsmithstore.com
Veneering supplies and some veneer

Woodworker's Supply
1108 North Glenn Road
Casper, WY 82601
1-800-321-9841
www.woodworker.com
Veneering supplies and some veneer

More Great Books from Fox Chapel Publishing

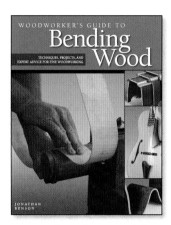

**Woodworker's Guide
to Bending Wood**
ISBN 978-1-56523-360-7 **$24.95**

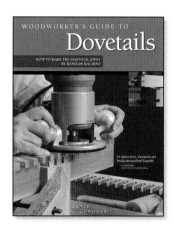

**Woodworker's Guide
to Dovetails**
ISBN 978-1-56523-387-4 **$24.95**

**Woodworker's & DIY Pocket
Guide, Second Edition**
ISBN 978-1-56523-811-4 **$14.99**

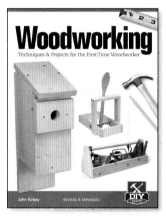

**Woodworking, Revised
and Expanded**
ISBN 978-1-56523-801-5 **$14.99**

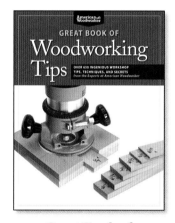

**Great Book of
Woodworking Tips**
ISBN 978-1-56523-596-0 **$24.95**

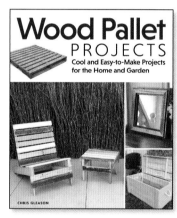

Wood Pallet Projects
ISBN 978-1-56523-544-1 **$19.99**

WOODCARVING ILLUSTRATED   SCROLLSAW woodworking &CRAFTS

In addition to being a leading source of woodworking books and
DVDs, Fox Chapel also publishes two premiere magazines. Released
quarterly, each delivers premium projects, expert tips and techniques
from today's finest woodworking artists, and in-depth information
about the latest tools, equipment, and materials.

Subscribe Today!
Woodcarving Illustrated: **888-506-6630**
Scroll Saw Woodworking & Crafts: **888-840-8590**
www.FoxChapelPublishing.com

Look for These Books at Your Local Bookstore or Specialty Retailer or at *www.FoxChapelPublishing.com*